FROM HEROIN

TO

MARATHON MOM

I would like to dedicate this book to my son Kingston James Stewart for changing my life and giving my life purpose. Mommy loves you more than you will ever know. I would also like to dedicate this to my mom, dad, sister and everyone else who never gave up on me.

Table of Contents

Introduction

Chapter 1: My Childhood

Chapter 2: Middle School

Chapter 3: 2003- Freshmen Year

Chapter 4: 2004- Sophomore Year

Chapter 5: The Summer I turned Sixteen

Chapter 6: 2005 Junior Year

Chapter 7: 2006- Senior Year

Chapter 8: 2007- The Year of Bad Luck

Chapter 9: 2007- Leading Up to my Felonies

Chapter 10: The Big Arrest

Chapter 11: They Got Me

Chapter 12: 2008- The Year of Court Dates

Chapter 13: My Four Month Prison Journey

Chapter 14: Life After Prison

Chapter 15: Addiction, Needles, and Lies

Chapter 16: Inpatient Treatment

Chapter 17: The Day I Died

Chapter 18: Fighting For My Life

Chapter 19: Pregnant

Chapter 20: Birth of my Son

Chapter 21: I am a New Mom

Chapter 22: The Beginning of Something New

Chapter 23: July 2012

Chapter 24: 2013- The Year of Marathons

Chapter 25: 2014- Going a New Distance

Chapter 26: Where I am at Today

Chapter 27: My Families Perspective

Epilogue

My Words of Advice

Introduction

Hi, my name is Jamie Stewart. Now you are probably wondering who I am and why I am writing a book. I am not a celebrity of any kind and I am far from a rock star. I am just your average ordinary girl. I am just an ordinary girl who happened to fight through the battle of addiction and make it out alive, barely.

I went from being a hollow shell of a human being to a bright and full of life human being. Before I was barely living and now I am living life to its fullest. I hit rock bottom and I kept on falling. Now I have reached the highest mountain and I keep on climbing.

So now you're probably wondering what is so great about Jamie's story? Why is her story better than anybody else? My story is not better or more exciting than anybody else's. I am writing my story to hopefully inspire people to break free from the chains of addiction. I want to inspire people to go after their goals and not let anything hold them back. I want to inspire people to dream big. All things are possible through hard work and perseverance. I am a living example of that. If I can help to inspire at least one person to make changes and do something better in life, then I am happy. Don't ever let anything or anyone hold you back from what you want to accomplish in life. Don't ever say you can't do it or it is too hard. It is possible to break free from addiction, but it is not easy. Anything in life worth fighting for is never easy. It is a lifelong commitment to stay clean but it is possible.

Before I do go into the story, I would like to thank my friends and family who stuck by my side and never gave up on me. They never lost hope in me and I am grateful that I have such a strong support system. Also, to my parents I am so sorry for everything I have done. I am so sorry for the things that I did that you didn't know I did and might just be learning. I did a lot of bad things and that is not who I am. It was out of my control and the addiction took over. You know that is not who I am today. I can't go back and change anything or fix anything, but from this day forward I am doing everything I can to be a better person. I am trying to make a better life for myself. My parents always did everything they could to help me, but there was nothing they could have done at the time. They instilled good morals in my head that stuck with me through my addiction. I always had a guilty conscience when I did things that I knew were bad. I love you mom and dad; I am so sorry for causing you so much pain.

So enough of me rambling on: let's cut right to the story. First you should know that this is all based off my life and it is all real. I do not want to sugar coat anything in my addiction but I will not use real names to protect identities. Also, there are certain things I will leave out for protection as well. It is not easy for me to write my story and I have put myself in a complete vulnerable state as I share it with you. I am releasing all of my inner demons and all of my deep, dark secrets. These are the facts of what it is like to be an addict and what my life has become after addiction. I really hope you enjoy this and I just pray that I can inspire people to get the help they need.

Chapter 1

My Childhood

I was born on June 17, 1988, to Richard and Diana Stewart in St. Charles, Missouri. I have one sister, Brittany, who is two and a half years older than me. We had a pretty normal childhood. My sister and I got along for the most part but we also had our fair share of sibling rivalry. To put things into perspective, my sister and I were polar opposites. She was a girly girl and I was a big tomboy. I was into sports and I dressed like a little boy. I also always hung out with all the boys.

I remember I always strived to be different from my family. For some reason I didn't want to like what they liked. If they liked something, I would say I didn't like it whether I did or not. They soon caught on to my little game and they began to say they didn't like certain things just so I would. I was always just a little different.

I grew up playing lots of sports and I swam on swim team all year round. My sister and I were both amazing swimmers and we always got the high point awards every year on our summer team. We also have a lot of first place ribbons. We traveled a lot for swim meets. My parents took us to all of our practices, games, and swim meets. I played a lot of different sports including soccer and softball. I also tried out a lot of different things such as tennis, basketball, and ice skating.

I did the kinds of things anyone would do growing up. My parents both worked and they never fought. We went on family vacations to Disney World and to California to visit our family. We lived in a nice neighborhood and a nice home. My parents instilled good values in my head. I was always super creative and smart. I loved to learn and I was always teacher's pet. I began reading at an earlier age than most kids and I had big dreams for the future. I always wanted to be a writer and it was something I always loved to do. When I was ten I wrote a book that I even tried to get published. I was always shy and terrified to get into trouble. I would get so nervous having to go to the office at school just to make a phone call to my mom that I would start crying. I was an extremely sensitive kid.

The majority of my childhood my grandmother lived with us. I was very close with her. She was like my best friend. She would always laugh at my sister and me when we got into trouble. It would always make my dad mad because we would start laughing. She is such an amazing lady and no words can describe her. She did tap dance for the St. Louis Strutters and I always bragged about her to everyone. She moved out around the time I was turning ten. I was devastated but she got an apartment not too far from us. I would stay with her on weekends sometimes. Shortly after she had moved, we put our house up on the market and we were moving. It wasn't too far from our old house.

I was going into fifth grade and my sister was in seventh grade. While our house was being built we moved into our grandmother's one bedroom apartment and she moved in with a friend for the time being. This was a rough time. There were four of us in a one bedroom, one bathroom apartment. It felt like the walls were closing in on us. My sister and I fought a lot during this time and my dad would always put us in time out. He would make us sit and stare at the wall and we always thought this was hilarious.

I became friends with an older lady down the hall. I would walk her dog, Frosty, to make money. I would also just go and hang out with her and talk. It gave me something to do to pass the time. It also got me out of that claustrophobic apartment.

We had to wake up extra early every morning so my mom could drop us off at school. My sister went to middle school and we would drop her off first. It started before my school so me and my mom would always have time to kill. Every morning we went to the King Burger on Highway K. It was one of the few places on Highway K at this time. We sat in the corner table and would go over my homework and sometimes eat breakfast as well. This memory is always funny to me because I have been working at that King Burger for nine years now.

I have mostly all good memories from my childhood. I do recall a couple of times where I did things that should have been red flags that I was just a little bit off. I was shy and just not very outspoken. I could get a bad temper if you set me off. There were fights that my sister and I got into that I know just aren't right. One time I beat the crap out of her with a shoe. I just wouldn't stop and I didn't care. She would make me mad. I also would chase her around the house with a big knife from the kitchen when she made me mad. That is not a normal thing to do. I did not plan to hurt her. I am not quite sure what my intentions were. I guess I just wanted to scare her. No big deal right? My mom came home one time and I had to hurry up and hide the knife. Of course, my sister told her and I got caught. Other than that my life was pretty normal. My sister and I had a bit of a rocky relationship during my addiction because of who I turned into. I am grateful for the relationship we have today. I love my sister a lot and I feel bad for everything I have done to her. I feel bad for putting her in the position she was in growing up while I went through my rough times. I don't feel it was fair to her.

So here is a piece of me growing up. By reading about my life growing up you may wonder what went wrong. I didn't go through any hardships growing up and everything was really pretty normal. So how did I end up getting caught up in drugs? It just goes to show that it can happen to anyone.

Chapter 2

Middle School

I think of middle school as you are just at that awkward age. It is different from elementary school but you are still that immature age. You haven't really established who you are as a person yet. You are just looking for some social acceptance.

I dressed like a little boy all through elementary school. My sister convinced me that I had to start dressing more girly. She would always pick out outfits for me and do my hair. I was not comfortable with how she dressed me. I would eventually develop my own style that changed throughout the years.

When I went into middle school I was just this quiet, shy, dorky little kid. I had frizzy red hair, freckles, and big messed up teeth. I just wanted to fit in. I met my best friend that year. We had every class together and her locker was right above mine. I finally found a group of friends who I felt like I belonged to. We would go to the mall and hang out on the weekends. We also had sleep overs every weekend. We would go to the school dances and the city hall dances. I was always too shy to dance at the dances. I was an extremely awkward kid. I began having crushes on boys but none of them ever seemed to like me.

I guess you could say we were a group of troublemakers. We just did random funny things. I started acting out in class and getting detentions. It wasn't like me or in my character, but I thought it made me cool. I thought getting into trouble made people like me. All I ever wanted to do was fit in, somehow, some way.

I think I was in seventh grade when I got my first boyfriend. It was a short lived relationship of about one month. My best friend at the time was going out with his best friend so we would all hang out together. I remember having our first kiss in the elevator at the mall. I can't recall exactly what happened, but we broke up. I remember him getting caught with a note I wrote him in class. I had got into trouble and called to the office for this note. I don't think that it was anything horrible, but it was inappropriate stuff for kids our age to be talking about. My principal called my parents and I got into trouble for it. I had to take it home to show them and to have them sign it. I didn't want to get into trouble so I said that I didn't write it. I told them it was somebody else who liked my boyfriend and was trying to get me into trouble. I wrote a fake note in a completely different hand writing to show my parents. They bought it. It was the beginning of my lies and deceitful behavior.

At some point in seventh grade, I developed a new group of friends. It wasn't anything that happened between me and my friends, but we just grew apart. We didn't have any classes together and we were on the opposite sides of the school. I got a new best friend and we were inseparable. Her name was Linda and we pretty much did all of the same stuff. We went to the mall and had sleep over parties. That is also when I met my friend Lisa. We all thought we were so awesome.

We were into emo/punk rock music. We even started playing instruments so we could start a band. I played the guitar and Linda played the bass. We were obsessed with Blink 182. We used to write songs and have band practices. We were always driven by money and trying to come up with new ways to make it. We used to sell burned CD's to our friends to make a little extra cash.

One year we went to Linda's dad's house in Chicago over the summer. We had a blast while we were there. I met some of her old friends who she had when she lived there. They were around the same age as us. I believe we were about thirteen at this time. Her friends were sitting around smoking cigarettes. I couldn't believe it! I had never been around anyone our age doing that. They could've been smoking pot too but I didn't know much about pot at this age. I was still pretty naïve to all of that. They asked if I wanted a drag off of a cigarette but I politely declined. My friend had taken a drag off of a cigarette and I wondered if I was supposed to also. Nobody tried to pressure me into it so I just stayed away from it. I always thought cigarettes were just absolutely disgusting.

It was the summer after my eighth grade year when I got drunk for the first time. I had just turned fourteen. I got ridiculously wasted and horribly sick. It was Linda, Lisa, and me over at Linda's house. Her parents were out of town for the weekend. I knew nothing about mixing alcohol but we were drinking Sky Blue Vodka and beer. I also smoked a cigarette that day. I was always so against smoking and I said I would never smoke. I used to always cough really loud when I would walk by people smoking in front of public places. I ended up getting sick and throwing up a lot that day. I was miserable and not sure why I ever drank again after that day. I was laying on the floor kicking the pole in her basement and for the longest time we referred to getting drunk as "kicking poles". I guess the joke is on me.

Due to my curious mind, I really wanted to try smoking pot. I am not sure why or what my reasons were. I guess I just thought it would make me cool and I wanted to be cool going into high school. I remember it was the summer after my eighth grade year. I was thirteen or fourteen at the time. I had bought a pipe and some pot off of a friend who I knew smoked pot. Linda and I decided to get

12

high together. I didn't know what I was doing. I just stuck some weed in the pipe and lit it up. We were posted up in a tunnel by the pond in my subdivision. I don't even know if I was high or not, mainly because I didn't know what to expect. I sure acted like I was.

So that was my first experience. Who knew it would lead to so much more. You always hear that pot is the gateway drug but you don't really believe it. I think a lot of it has to do with who you surround yourself with. I always had a curious mind so I always wanted to try new things. I was always looking for acceptance and I just wanted to fit in. I was never comfortable in my own skin and becoming a druggie I never had to worry about that. I always battled depression and drugs helped with that. At least I always thought it did, but it really just made me feel worse. I didn't realize I had such an addictive personality. This was just the beginning. And on to high school we go. This is where all the fun begins.

Chapter 3

2003- Freshmen Year

Here comes the real story of when a lot of stuff began. I am going to try to replay everything as it happened and keep it in the best order that I can. In general, my life was out of order. I began my freshmen year of high school at Fort Zumwalt West High School. It sucked because the majority of my friends went to South High because of where we lived. I went into school feeling alone, but at least my sister also went there. The school was huge and I felt scared and like a fly on the wall. I was fourteen when I began my freshmen year. I was always the youngest in my grade since my birthday was in the summer.

When I first began high school, I was still a bit of a goodie two shoes. I had dabbled in a couple things, but I was not yet a troubled teenager. I played softball my freshmen year, but I didn't like it too much after that. I began to make new friends and I didn't care about any extra- curricular activities anymore. I cared more about hanging out with my friends. After one season of softball, I had quit all sports. That was when my troubles began.

Since my sister also went to school with me and she was older, I at least got to ride to school with her. I was so nervous going into school and felt like I didn't know anyone. Once I made friends, I ended up riding to school with them instead of my sister. At this time, I had not started smoking pot heavily yet. Sometimes my friends and I would get salvia because they sold it at a store in the mall. It was the big thing back then but it was kind of dumb. I can't explain the high from it, but you smoked it and it looked similar to pot. Once I made new friends, I started smoking pot every day. I would always smoke before school. I very rarely went to school not stoned. If I had to ride with my sister, I would smoke in the garage before we left. My sister would tell me I was a pot head, but I never really thought of myself as a pot head. I thought I was just a normal teenager. I always had Spanish first hour and I was not good at it which could have been because I was always under the influence.

I remember I started partying a lot more around this time. Every weekend I was going out drinking, partying, and smoking pot. My parents gave me a curfew of midnight, but that didn't go over so well with me. All my friends had later curfews or no curfews at all, so I would usually end up spending the night at friends' houses. When my parents told me I couldn't stay the night at a friend's house, I would just do it anyways. I would also sneak out a lot after they went to sleep. One time my friend and I were trying to sneak out my basement window. When we pulled the window forward, it shattered. There was broken glass everywhere. I ended up having to make up a story about that one. I am sure my parents didn't believe me, but they went along with it anyways. I was disrespectful to my parents at this time. I had the whole, "You're not the boss of me and I don't give a damn" attitude. They were beginning to get worried about me. Also, my grades began to slip, not because I wasn't smart but because I didn't care about school anymore.

Due to my behavior and acting out so much between home and school, my parents thought I had a problem. I was skipping school, my grades were slipping, and I was just showing all of the signs of a troubled teenager. I remember going to lots of doctors for depression and anxiety. I can't recall whether I brought up drugs and alcohol at the doctor's yet. I know at one point my parents had me drug tested. My parents would show the doctors my dark writings and journal entries. I would write entries about how much I hated life and how much I hated my parents. I was prescribed

Adderall and some anti-depressants. The first one I took was Zoloft, but I went through a lot of different ones. I loved the way the Adderall made me feel. It was just like speed to me and I enjoyed it. I manipulated my way into getting that one. I would sometimes sell it to my friends or just give it away. When I started taking it my GPA went from a 2.0 to a 3.0. I would stay up all night or days at a time and I would hardly eat.

Things began to get worse. I was really heading down the wrong path, but I just didn't care. I just thought that I was a bad ass and I didn't really care what anyone else thought of me. Sometimes I would get drunk before school or we would just skip and get drunk at home. I didn't care about school at all anymore and I was just going for the social aspect. My parents knew I was headed down the wrong path and they tried to intervene but nothing was working at this time. I would continue to do as I pleased. I would sometimes get detentions, which I would hardly ever go to. That would usually end up with me being in the in school suspension program and occasionally out of school suspensions. I felt like out of school suspensions were a reward.

I had my first boyfriend in high school when I was fourteen. His name was Josh and it was a friend of a friend of mine. He told my friend he thought I was cute, so she gave him my number. One night we stayed up all night talking on the phone. It was a short relationship and I believe we were only together for about one month. Everything seemed good while it lasted and I thought he liked me. Looking back at it now, I realize he was not nice to me. He cheated on me twice and I stayed. I will also never forget when he told me I was the only girl he'd ever been with who had love handles. I didn't even know what that meant at first but soon figured out he was basically telling me I was fat. I didn't have the best self esteem to begin with and it plummeted after that. Luckily, taking Adderall suppressed my appetite, so I hardly ate after that. This was kind of my first experience at a relationship. I know it wasn't long, but it was definitely a memory. As weird as it sounds, I liked being treated like shit. I think it was because I didn't think highly of myself and I just wanted to be accepted. I would do anything for acceptance and I was that nice girl who got taken advantage of, always.

I had my first job when I was fourteen. I worked at an Italian restaurant bussing tables. I am pretty sure I was working illegally. I was so young and I didn't even have a worker's permit. I was also getting paid under the table. I would use all of my cash to buy shoes and pot. I think I owned every pair of DC shoes they made at the time. I can't remember exactly how long I worked there, but I would say close to six months. I started smoking pot more and more working there. I worked with a lot of older people who also influenced me. I also remember the Christmas party they had. Now remember I was only fourteen at this point and they had an open bar. Just because it is an open bar doesn't mean somebody of my age should be drinking. Well, I got absolutely wasted. I remember my sister picking me up. I can't remember too many details other than I was really drunk.

I used to always ride my bike or skateboard to my friends' houses that lived nearby. I would use my lunch money to buy pot and alcohol. My friend and I would split the cost and we would always hangout at his house since his mom was always gone.

My freshmen year was just the beginning of my troubles. Looking back, I realize how hard it was being a teenager. I was looking to fit in and I didn't know who I was. I battled depression and I didn't deal with the big crowds of high school very well. People could be so mean and there was so much unnecessary drama. I tried to stay out of it all. I was always laid back, but maybe because I was always high. I hated going to school, but I did love all the parties and the people I met.

Chapter 4

2004- Sophomore Year

By this point, not very much has changed. Things just began to get worse as I made more friends to get into trouble with. I didn't care too much about anyone or anything, myself included. I was fifteen years old and going into my sophomore year. I hung out with a lot of people in the grade above me. By this point, I was skipping school more often. I usually would go until third hour and leave out the side door. Sometimes I would skip my fourth hour and go to all three of the lunches to hang out with my friends. It looked weird on my report card when my fourth hour had so many more absences than my other classes.

I began working at the Mack's Burger in the mall. Since I was only fifteen, I could only work weekends and had to be off by a certain time. My friend Brittany helped me get the job there. When I began working there, I had only smoked pot and drank alcohol. I am not sure if I had tried any other drugs yet. While working there, I met a new group of friends to hang out with. This was the time when I really started to party more and try new things. I remember I would always go hang out with the boys, skateboard, and smoke pot. I began to learn more and more about drugs and ways to get high. One night I was hanging out with some people from work and I smoked meth for the first time. It was the second drug I had ever tried. That was the only time I ever did that. After this, though, I began trying more things.

Every weekend we would hang out at friend's houses. We spent a lot of time hanging out in my friend's garage and if we weren't there, we were in another friend's shed. I would spend the night at Brittany's house every weekend and she would drive me to work in the morning. We always stayed out all night and I knew if I went home my parents would make me go home earlier. One weekend, I decided to drink a bottle of Robitussen cough syrup because I heard if you did a bunch of it then it would make you trip. I was always looking for ways to get high. It was true. I was tripping. I was in my own world and I thought things were there that really weren't. I remember watching cartoons on the wall. I had to work the next day and I am not sure what happened, but my eyes were completely blood shot. They didn't get better with eye drops and I had to work with my eyes like that. At work, all the customers were just staring at me and some made comments. My eyes stayed like that for a couple of days. I even had to go to school like that where my teachers made comments. I had to tell my parents that I thought I had some kind of eye infection. My principal from school had even contacted my mom and told her what she thought it was. I don't remember what happened or if my parents even talked to me about it. I do know that this situation was not fun.

I will never forget one day when Brittany and I decided to skip school. We had the best day ever just running around and having fun. We went to breakfast and then went to St. Louis Mills Mall. I remember everything from this day. We came back to my house since my parents were at work. It was about one minute until the time school actually let out when my garage opened. We were sitting at the counter in my kitchen painting glass mushrooms we had bought from the Goodwill. My dad walked in the door and I had the look of a deer caught in the headlights. Of course, my dad looked at the clock and questioned what we were doing. I made up a lie that school got let out early. He called the school and caught me in my lie. We had friends call the school to excuse our absences so they found out when my dad called. My dad made Brittany leave and he and I got in an argument. I had a bad attitude and I was disrespectful. I ended up getting grounded for the weekend. I packed a bag of stuff and I planned to run away. I waited until my dad went down into the basement. I gave it a few minutes to make sure it was clear. I grabbed my skate board and my book bag and I quietly slipped out the front door. I made a break for it and I didn't look back.

I skated to one of my friend's houses not too far away. I was laughing at the fact I had escaped and we celebrated by smoking pot. It wasn't long before my parents were blowing up my phone and trying to figure out where I was. I kept ignoring the calls but they weren't giving up. I think I eventually answered the phone and told them to leave me alone. I ended up having Brittany come pick me up. I went over to my Grandmother's house for the weekend and I stayed with her. She took me to work over the weekend and eventually come Sunday, I had to go home. It was time to face my parents.

I had run away one other time. I wrote my parents a big, long note basically telling them I was sick of them and I needed a break. I told them that I didn't like the way they treated me. It is crazy to look back at all of this now and see how ridiculous I acted. So I wrote them a long note and told them I was going to live with Brittany for a little while. They didn't like this considering I was only fifteen. I guess legally they wouldn't allow it. I always threatened to move out the day I turned eighteen which is funny because I am still living at home. I went to Brittany's house and they wouldn't leave us alone. They came over and sat outside of her house until I finally came home. It was not a good time and in the time I was gone they searched my room. They found my stash of paraphernalia. I can't remember what it was I had, maybe just a pipe or two.

I was an extremely depressed teenager. I hated life and I didn't want to be alive. I wanted to take the easy way out. I used to always plan out my death. I would write suicide notes and take a bunch of pills in hopes that I would not wake up. I would lay the notes on a pillow next to me as I lay down to go to sleep. I always woke up. As much as I wanted to take my own life, I was scared. I wanted to take the easy way out but I could never go through with it. I would try, but in reality I intentionally never took enough to actually die. If I really would have wanted to, well then I would have. I still have all of the suicide notes that I wrote. Most of them are ridiculous. I am thankful that I never did take my life.

My parents continued to try getting help. They tried to give me rules, but I wouldn't follow them. If they wanted me to be home by a curfew, then I would come home drunk. They would wait up for me to make sure I came home. There I was fifteen and wasted. I would try to blame them for my actions. It was because they wouldn't give me freedom. It was all their fault. They took me to counselors and tried doing drug tests. Whenever they drug tested me, I would quit smoking pot. That is when I tried other drugs that would get out my system faster. This was when I really started getting into harder drugs such as ecstasy and cocaine.

They used to give me money for my grades. They owed me two hundred dollars for getting good grades but they waited until a day when my sister and I were going shopping. They thought that would help control the money and what I spent it on. A few days prior to them giving me my money, I found two hundred dollars in an old purse of my mom's. I stole that money thinking it was mine and a couple of days later they gave me my money. I don't think my parents even know about that (sorry mom and dad). So here I had four hundred dollars, what was I to do with all this money? I bought a quarter pound of weed from a friend. I and sit was easy to get my hands on large amounts of weed. Since I wasn't really smoking at this time, I sold it to make money. That was me trying to beat the system. It was also my first experience at drug dealing. I enjoyed flipping it and making more money. It gave me a rush.

I was eating a lot of ecstasy at this time as well. They were colorful little pills that I would swallow or snort. We referred to being high on ecstasy as "rolling". I had bought some pills off of someone and I was planning to eat some and sell a few. My parents had found the pills in my room and ended up taking me to a late night counseling session. It was cutting into my plans of rolling that night and I didn't even know they had found them. I was trying to get out of that session as quickly as I could so I could go party. Finally, I got home and I was getting ready to go out and roll with my friends. I went to grab my pills from where I had left them and that is when I realized they were missing. I flipped out. I yelled at my parents for taking them. I told them they had no right to take them and that I was just holding them for a friend. They weren't mine and if I didn't get them back to their rightful owner I would die. I ended up leaving with my friend and we went and bought some more pills so we could get messed up that night. That was a crazy night. We ended up in an awkward situation at some stranger's house. I don't even know how we met them or ended up there but those were the kind of things I always got myself into. I finally made it back home the next day feeling like I got run over by a bus. My parents were at work, so I searched their room for my pills. I found them and I ended up selling them. I slept that whole day to recover. My parents found out I took them and I told them I had to give them back so I didn't get killed.

I also ate a lot of mushrooms at this time. I never really planned things through as to where I would go and what I would do. I had some good trips and some bad trips. I went to a friend's house one day to buy some mushrooms, so I just ate them there. I thought we were all going to be hanging out and tripping together. They ended up having something to do and they dropped me off on the side of 7-11. The sun was still out and I sat on the side of the building tripping for awhile. I couldn't get a hold of anyone at first. Many customers came in and out of the store. I am sure I looked like I was up to no good. I even had some people ask me if I needed help. I kindly turned down any offers for help. I was just sitting there and I wasn't causing any trouble. Finally I got a hold of someone to come pick me up and we went over to her boyfriend's house. I was so thankful she came to my rescue. I remember driving and wondering why there were dogs driving cars. At her boyfriend's house we ended up getting more messed up. I ate a bunch of valium and drank some beer. I remember being up most the night and my eyes rolling into the back of my head. It was yet another crazy night and I always wonder how I am even still alive.

About halfway through the school year, I was going to drop out of school. I was pretty much failing most of my classes anyways by this point. I was never at school and I skipped more days than I went to. I was going to try out home schooling. I withdrew from my classes, but I had also put in an application at the alternative school. I had to go through an interview process and I did not think I was going to get accepted. It was a small school and there were only about one hundred kids in the school. Everyone always made fun of the school calling it "dope high" and saying there's still hope. It was over Christmas break when I got the call and found out I got accepted. I was so happy and I loved my high school. They did more hands on learning and I loved the smaller class sizes. I felt like I could actually learn. Most importantly, I was there every day; well for the most part. If you missed a certain amount of hours, you would have to make it up on certain days at payback time.

I remember on my second day at my new school I got in trouble for wearing a billabong hoodie because it just said bong across it. I thought it was random, but apparently the teachers had mentioned it at the school meeting. I missed that part, but it had to do with representing drugs, even though it was just a brand of clothing. I also remember getting in trouble one day for wearing a pacifier around my neck. I didn't think anyone would know what it symbolized, especially not my teachers. It was a reference to eating ecstasy and my teacher pulled my in the hall and made me take it off.

Since it was the alternative school, we didn't have buses to take us. I rode with a girl named Mary who lived nearby. I would usually smoke before school or we would smoke together on the way. I felt bad because I would wake up late a lot and Mary would be on the driveway honking. One day I was at school and I left my phone in her car. Some girl in my second hour was talking about some guy named Charles who had gone to West High that passed away. She said the name but she wasn't positive on the last name, so I tried not to freak out too much. I corrected her on the name and asked if that was right. She said "Yea that's it." I am pretty sure my face turned pale. It was a good friend of mine and the first person I was close to that I lost. He was only nineteen and he had gotten into a car accident. I dealt with it the same way I dealt with anything: I got messed up. I went to the funeral, but I had a hard time dealing with it since it was my first real experience with death. He was one of the nicest people you could meet. He was friends with everyone.

So here I am fifteen years old and I am headed down a completely self destructive path. I did not think I was that bad. I thought this was what any normal teenager did. If you weren't doing what I was doing, then I thought you were weird. I mean all my friends were doing it. One thing led to another and I was trying everything. I was eating ecstasy, Dramamine, drinking, taking pain pills, smoking pot, snorting cocaine, and just a little bit of everything. I would take up to fifty Dramamine pills at a time. When I would take pain pills, I would take up to ten of them and I would drink on top of all this. I was also eating mushrooms, acid and Xanax. I didn't think I was doing anything wrong. I thought this was normal for everyone my age to do these things. I was still working at the Mack's Burger in the mall and all of my money went to drugs. You will probably hear me say this a lot, but I still don't know how I managed to live through all of this. The fact I am alive today is a miracle. I thought I was invincible.

Chapter 5

The Summer I Turned Sixteen

I got my license the day I turned sixteen. I was so excited and I felt like I had freedom. My sister and I would share a car for a little while. I felt like now I could really do whatever I wanted. I got the car pretty often but not always when I wanted to. My parents didn't know that I smoked cigarettes yet. I always smelled like them but I blamed my friends. My friends convinced me to smoke in my car and if I rolled the windows down the smell would go away. That didn't work so well. My sister found a lighter I dropped in the car and I got caught. She told on me. I always got caught.

When I was sixteen, I went through a really bad stage with duster. Duster is the cans of air that you use to clean computers and electronics. I would inhale it. Don't ask why. It was really stupid but I had an obsession with it. My friends and I would go to Wal-Zones and steal duster every day. We would literally go through a couple of cans a day. Sometimes I would take puffs off of the can inside the store and walk around. It was a quick, short high that is hard to even explain. There were times where I blacked out and fell out. I remember doing it outside of a friend's house late one night and falling backwards. I remember my head bouncing off of the concrete and waking up to everyone yelling my name. My head hurt horribly after that. One time we were sitting in a parking lot doing it and I passed out hanging halfway out of my car. I wonder what people thought when they walked by. There was also once when I did it while I was driving and I passed out at the wheel. Luckily, it wasn't for very long. I still wonder how I am alive. I was so stupid and that is just pure stupidity. One day I had a can of duster in my purse. I had puffed some of it before going to bed and I just left it in my purse. My sister found a lighter in her car so she came into my room while I was still sleeping. She searched my purse looking for cigarettes but instead she found the can of duster. She told my parents on me. I am surprised I am not completely brain damaged from the amount of duster that I did.

I was completely disrespecting my parents at this time and they were at a loss on what to do. My sister would try to get them to realize that I was up to no good. It made her so mad that I would just get away with everything. I was always good at getting my way. My parents ended up putting my in an outpatient rehab in St. Louis. My sister would drive me to a majority of my classes and I would drive myself sometimes. I didn't take the classes seriously and I was not happy about having to go there. I was ignorant to the teachers and I had a closed mind. I didn't quit smoking pot for this one and they would always give me drug test. I would tell them that I smoke pot and I didn't care. I wouldn't stop and they couldn't make me stop. Due to the fact it was also a mental health center, you had to get a key to unlock the bathroom doors. I will never forget going in there after a night of drinking and being hung over. I had been throwing up and I was throwing up in the bushes before I even made it into the center. Then, I went in and I was going to get the keys to the bathroom. Nobody was at the front desk to get me the keys. I couldn't wait, so I was going to run outside. I had to walk down a flight of stairs to get there. I was about five steps from the bottom when I just projectile vomited all down the steps. I just left it and didn't tell anyone. I didn't go to that rehab for too long and it obviously wasn't helping. I believe it was about a month or so that I went there. I did stay talking with a counselor, just not through the outpatient classes.

When I first started driving I was not a good driver. I was just scared and careful. I will never forget one day these guys needed a ride to Wentzeville. It was a very far drive from where we were, but they said they would give me cocaine if I did it. I was scared to drive, but of course I said yes since I was getting drugs. It didn't help my driving since it was dark out and I had to drive on the highway. I remember going to get on the highway and a semi truck was coming. I slammed on my breaks instead of speeding up and merging. The guys in my car yelled at me and they were not nice about it. We were all scared to death. The rest of the ride went better and when we got there, they gave me a big line of coke. That made it all worth it.

I remember a lot from this summer. We had a lot of parties and a lot of fun. A lot of my friends were homeless at the time because their parents would kick them out. I would always try to sneak my friends in but I would always get caught. I would be trying to sneak in three guys at a time. Sometimes I would get caught sneaking them in and sometimes I would get caught the next day trying to sneak them out. My grandmother was staying in California for a few months with family. My parents had a key to her apartment so one day I went and made a copy of the key so a friend of mine would have a place to stay. Of course, I got caught after he stayed there one or two nights. My grandmother was very upset with me and I still feel bad about that to this day. My grandmother was my best friend and I disrespected her. I completely betrayed her. It hurt to have my grandmother so disappointed in me because she was one person I never wanted to hurt.

I had quit my job at the Mack's in the mall since I could drive now. I was going to get a different job. I didn't get a new job right away, but shortly after. I worked a few different jobs for a little bit at a time. I worked at a pizzeria for about a day. I worked at a bagel shop for a few days. I think I also worked somewhere else in there and then I started working at Drive Inn's as a cook. My best friend Brittany also worked there. We had another job together. Actually, quite a few of my friends worked there at the time which made it fun. Brittany would always make fun of me because I was always serious about working. I have always been a good worker and had a good work ethic. Yes, throughout some of my addiction I screwed places over, but I would rarely call off no matter how sick I was.

I used to shop lift from a lot of places. I would go to Wal-Zones a lot or I would steal alcohol from grocery stores. I know that it was stupid. One day I decided to go with a friend to J-Mart to steal some items for her. I always went to Wal-Zones so I decided to switch it up a little bit. That was a bad idea because they actually have security there to sit and watch the cameras. As I was leaving the store, a guy stopped me and made me go to the back with him. I had never felt so nervous. They didn't call the cops because they said otherwise they would always have the cops there. Instead, they made me call my parents. I tried to make up a story about my parents being gone but they wouldn't let me leave unless my parents picked me up. I had to have them come get me. That was an awkward drive home. I never had to go to court or anything. I just had to pay a fine. I was scared to shop lift after that, so I guess you could say I learned my lesson.

I will never forget the first time I got pulled over and got my first ticket. We were at a friend's house and we had all eaten ecstasy. There were five of us and we were all messed up, including me who was driving. We all decided to hop into my car and go to Mack's Burger to get food. We all had pacifiers and light up toys. Oh and it was three in the morning. It wasn't a real far drive so I figured we would be fine. We didn't make it far and I saw flashing lights behind me. I thought they looked cool and I just stared at them. I was so nervous, I was shaking. We all just looked suspicious. We just looked like a bunch of kids up to no good. The officer searched the car but did not find any drugs. He ended up giving me a ticket for being out past curfew. I was lucky nothing worse happened but I still had to somehow tell my parents. I waited until right before my court date to tell them. I was good at waiting until the last minute.

Chapter 6

2005- Junior Year

The amazing summer came to an end and it was time to go back to school. My sister had her own car now so I got the beat up Dodge Neon. It was nice being able to drive myself to school and I would carpool with friends sometimes as well. We would always smoke pot before school. I think, the teachers would question it more if I came to school not high.

I was kind of a bit crazy and a bit of a class clown. On Halloween, I wore a superman costume to school. I had found the costume in the little boy's section at Goodwill and I just had to have it. Everyone got a kick out of the costume and my picture even made the yearbook along with our Power point collage at our graduation ceremony. I decided to quit my job at Drive Inn's and the day I went to quit, I wore my superman costume to tell my manager. I thought I was hilarious and clever, but not all adults found me funny.

When I was sixteen, I was still a virgin. Everyone was having sex and I had some close calls, but I was too scared. I finally decided it was time to see what all the fuss was about. My friend set me up with this one guy. We had been hanging out and I thought he was cute and of course my friend told him. I figured why not? What did I have to lose? I mean other than my virginity. We basically planned it out. His name was Alex and he was a few years older than me. We never had a relationship. We just had sex a few times. One night we drank a bunch of Southern Comfort and went to his house. It was on sheets laid out in his basement, how romantic. I thought the more Southern Comfort I drank, the less it would hurt. It didn't feel that good the first time and I was sore the next day. I still tried it again though. We had sex a few more times and that was it. After that, I slept with a few more guys but none of them were relationships, just hook ups. Not too long after that I did end up getting into my first real, long term relationship. When I was not in relationships I would live the life of: sex, drugs, and rock n' roll. I became rather promiscuous and I had no respect for myself.

I ended up getting a job at another Mack's, just not the one in the mall. It was right by all of my friend's houses which made it convenient. I would usually go in right after school. I worked with a lot of cool people and met some new friends. This is where I met my soon to be boyfriend, Joe. I will get to that story shortly as it was over a year and a half of my life.

I started working there around Christmas time. I remember one evening a friend of mine and I went to get piercings. I was going to get my eyebrow pierced and she was going to get her tongue pierced. I was only sixteen so, of course, you can't go to a shop and legally get it done. I knew my parents would flip out, but I loved getting a rise out of them. I got my eyebrow pierced one night in this guy's apartment. I loved it. I had to bandage it up at work and I hid it from my parents for a week. Everyone always ask how I did that. It was easy. I hid it with my hair and with a hat. Plus I wasn't around my parents too much anyway. I tried not to be. It was Christmas morning when my sister and I went down to open presents. I had my black spitfire beanie with a bill on it cocked to the side. It was pulled down and covering my piercing. My mom told me to take it off so I would look decent for photos. I said, "Okay, but you are not going to like what you see."

"Why?" shouted my dad.

I took the hat off and they flipped out, just as I expected they would. Their first reaction was who did this. You're not old enough to get this done. They wanted to know who was responsible, but I refused to tell them. They wanted to get him in trouble, but I wouldn't allow it. It kind of ruined that Christmas. I was always good at ruining everything. It was a huge fight and my parents threatened to take back all of my gifts. They made me take it out. I would take it out and put something back in it anytime I left the house. They eventually gave in and let me keep it in. They knew it was a battle they were going to lose. I always won everything. They just made me a deal that I had to take it out anytime we were around a bunch of family, especially my grandma.

Now let's talk about that boy I met. We worked at Mack's Burger together. His name was Joe and he was a couple of years older than me. The story of when we began dating is really pretty funny. He was a bit of a preppy boy and I was a total skater chick, a little rough around the edges. I had a lot of piercings and my ears gauged out. I had thought he was cute and we would flirt a lot. One night he was working an overnight and me and my friend had gone through the drive thru. We were all messed up. We had drank a bunch and taken a lot of Xanax. The manager let him come out and he came outside and sat in the car with us. At some point in the conversation we became boyfriend and girlfriend. I just didn't really remember and I blame the Xanax for that. In fact, I didn't even realize we were together until a week or so later. He was talking about going to prom and I didn't realize we were together. Whoops!

We had an incredibly weird relationship. We were together around two years. A lot happened in this time so I will trying piecing it together the best that I can. This was a huge part of my high school days. He was the first person I ever said "I love you" to. I felt so in love. Our biggest problem was that we were both so jealous and insecure. We were both a bit crazy. In the beginning, we were super happy. My friends didn't like him very much because he was controlling. They hated the fact he tried forcing me to quit smoking cigarettes. He did succeed at that but we would both smoke when we were messed up. My friends didn't think I was around enough anymore and I was spending too much time with him. We were a package deal and we were pretty much inseparable. The majority of our fights were over us being jealous. I didn't like him talking to girls and he didn't like me talking to any guys. The majority of my friends were boys and he didn't like me hanging out with them.

We had a lot of good times together and a lot of bad times together. We began going to a lot of festivals together. We were both driven by money and would sell drugs to make extra money. It also gave us an opportunity to not pay for our drugs. He didn't have a car so I would let him take my car to use while I was at work so he could take care of business. We would have people meet us at work a lot. I will never forget the first time we got pulled over together. We had come back from a festival not that long before that and we had all kinds of drugs in the car. We were leaving the gas station and on our way to his house. We got pulled over as we turned into his subdivision. The reasoning was that my license plate light was out. While we were getting pulled over, Joe was stuffing all of the drugs into our hiding spots. The air vents in my car popped out and we were able to shove everything in there. We had our pipe, weed, mushrooms, mesculine and I believe we also had ecstasy. I was so nervous, but we managed to get it all hidden before being searched. It was way too close of a call and I knew we needed to be more careful.

Every weekend we were partying at friends' houses and getting drunk. Sometimes the alcohol would bring us closer

35

together and sometimes it would turn into huge fights. Nobody enjoyed being around us when we had our drunken fights. I mean really who would want to be around that? I usually stayed the night at his house a lot on the weekends. We spent a lot of time driving around and smoking pot. I always went through phases with certain drugs. In the beginning of our relationship I remember it was a Xanax phase. I was getting endless supplies of Xanax and I loved taking it. Also from time to time we would eat acid. I will never forget the time we stayed up all night tripping acid and I stayed at his house. Early the next morning, when we were still up from the night before, we decided it was a good idea to drive out to the Wentzeville flea market. We got ready and we drove all the way there. We parked in the parking lot and took a look at each other and realized we were frying. There was no way we could walk around and look normal. We drove all the way back to his house in hopes we would get back before his parents were up. Then we ran down to his room and we hid out.

I can't remember much else that really stands out about my junior year. I was going to Hope High School, taking correspondence courses and taking night school classes to make up credits when I withdrew from my other school. I spent my weekends partying and getting drunk. I sold pot to make extra cash and I was also smoking a large amount of pot. I ate a lot of Xanax, acid and ecstasy. That summer we went to about every festival they had. I would tell my parents I was going camping. I would stay up eating endless amounts of drugs, camping and listening to good music. It was the most peaceful thing ever and it would usually take me a few days to fully recover from the lack of sleep and the amount of drugs I would eat. I snorted so much ecstasy that every time I blew my nose, it was rainbow colored snot for days. I was just being a normal teenager, right?

Chapter 7

2006- Senior Year

Not very much had changed from my junior year to my senior year. I was still doing the same things, same school, same job and same boyfriend. I am seventeen now and I still think "my shit don't stink". I had a couple run ins with the law, but nothing ever happened. It was just times I would get pulled over, maybe searched but the police never found anything. Joe and I would get a long for the most part but we would also fight, break up, and threaten to kill ourselves. I told you we were both a bit crazy. We were just young and insecure.

Joe and I did celebrate our one year anniversary during my senior year. We had a big night planned for our anniversary. We had gotten a hotel room and our friends bought us some ecstasy pills to celebrate. It would always bring us closer together and make us feel more in love than ever. Ecstasy tends to have that affect. Even your worst enemies are your best friends when you are rolling. We stayed up all night rolling and just enjoying each other's company. We had a couple friends stop by to hang out with us throughout the night. It was an unforgettable night.

I only had to go half of my senior year and I graduated early. I had made up a lot of credits with my correspondence and my night school. It's funny because I didn't think I would end up graduating and I am pretty sure most of my family didn't expect it either. Then I ended up graduating early. If it wasn't for going to Hope, I am not sure I would've graduated. It was the only place I felt like I belonged and my teachers were awesome. I formed some unforgettable bonds.

I had quit my job at Mack's Burger. I forget exactly how I quit but I know I didn't do it in a mature way. It was me being immature and not liking my manager. I got a job working at Michael's for a little bit but I really didn't like it. It was too slow pace and boring for me. That is when I got hired on at King Burger. It was around March of 2006. Since I was no longer in school, I began working days. It was rough in the beginning. Some days I liked it and some days I hated it. It didn't help that I was always partying. I drank so much I hardly even got hangovers and I was taking Adderall to keep me awake and motivated at work.

One night Joe and I were driving around hanging out with friends. He had accidentally dialed his parent's number while his phone was in his pocket and they heard our whole conversation about drugs. They made us go there and we had to sit down and talk with them. That was awkward, especially since we had just got done driving around and smoking. His parents ended up kicking him out of his house. That was a really bad time for us. I talked my parents into letting him come stay with us for a little while. He ended up staying with us for about a month. He had to stay in the guest bedroom, but I would sneak him in my room to sleep after my parents went to bed. This was a test for our relationship. We fought a lot during this time period and I know a lot of it was because we got no space. I also felt like it was an invasion of my personal space. I remember I hadn't been working at King Burger long and I had to go in there one Saturday. I will never forget this day. Joe and I had got into a huge fight right before I had to go to work. I was crying and upset but tried to pull it together since I had just started my job. We were so busy that day and I couldn't focus on work but I had to. I was so afraid Joe was going to do something to hurt himself since he had threatened it.

I had my graduation ceremony at school in May. My parents were so proud of me. My school put together an amazing ceremony. I will never forget that day and I can't describe how awesome it felt. I was bummed because all of my friends were going to a festival the weekend we graduated. I couldn't go because all of my family was in town for my graduation and we had my party that weekend. I still celebrated and got wasted with a bunch of other friends. We spent that summer going to more festivals every weekend that there was one. Joe and I were still together but it still went back and forth with our fights. We were too comfortable to just leave each other and start over. It was my first long term relationship and my first "love."

We broke up for good at some point after the Summer. I do not know an exact time line of what happened or what our breaking point was. We were broken up but we still saw each other at parties and social gatherings. We had a lot of the same friends. I had a couple hook ups here and there. I started kind of talking to someone new but it made Joe mad. He didn't know we were talking but he assumed it. His name was Aaron and he was a little older than me. He was super nice and really awesome. I feel bad because I was just young and immature. I couldn't commit myself to any type of relationship as I didn't know what I wanted. I messed up on this one. Anyway, Joe and I were broken up but we would still hangout and hook up sometimes. We hung out on New Year's Eve and we went to a party together. While we were there he happened to see a text that Aaron had sent me. It basically said something about a kiss at midnight. Even though Joe and I were not together, it pissed him off. It didn't help that he was drunk. I actually didn't drink very much this night because I was driving and I had to work the next day.

Eventually Joe and I left the party we were at and everything from there went downhill. I drove him to his car and we parted ways. I planned to go to Aaron's to hangout for a little while. I stared driving and went a different way home than what I normally would. Joe called me and asked me why I went that way. I just said I felt like it. I went over to Aaron's and wasn't hanging out there for long when Joe called because he was out front. It was a bad situation. Joe was drunk and caused a huge scene where we got into a fight. Aaron and his friends stepped in to keep Joe from getting physical with me. It ended in a huge fist fight and Joe got his ass kicked and then called the cops. He was bleeding everywhere and I was unfortunately forced to go with him. I can't remember what happened with Joe. I think he may have gone to hospital. I know the officers made me blow to check my blood alcohol levels and I had to drive his car home and have my parents come pick me up. Aaron and his friends ended up with court dates and fines. I felt so bad that they had to go through that. I tried to have a nice relaxed New Year's so I would feel good at work the next day. Instead, I had to deal with this huge mess.

After that, we stayed apart for good, although I still think we had jealousy issues and would occasionally hook up. I talked to Aaron for a little bit but I just couldn't commit. I had a lot to deal with. I started drinking a lot of alcohol at this point and I was selling pot on my own, without Joe. I was never careful about it since I couldn't just have pot lying around at my house. It was a lot harder on my own. So this brings us into the year 2007. I was eighteen at this time. This is where all my trouble begins, literally.

Chapter 8

2007- The Year of Bad Luck

They always say bad things or good things come in three. I never believed that but it seems to be true. The year of 2007 was not my lucky year. It is where all my troubles began with the law. I am not sure why I waited until I was eighteen to get in trouble. I mean with all the bad things I did as a minor, I would've rather gotten in trouble then!

It was a cold, winter day in January. I was young and free, not a care in the world. I remember just hanging out with my friends all day, drinking a little booze and smoking a whole lot of marijuana. The person I was hanging out with, well, it was blunts all day. I was beyond high and I think the smell of marijuana seeped into my skin. That night, we went to a friends to play beer pong and just hangout. We continued to do the same things, drink and smoke. It had been a long day. For some reason, we came up with the grand idea to go to get greasy breakfast food at two in the morning, probably not the best idea when you have been drinking and smoking all day.

We all piled into my friend's car, five deep. We were going to get some drunken munchies. What could possibly go wrong? We went and ate some food, and then headed back to my friends house. We were literally two streets over from making it back to our destination. Some car was riding on my friend's tail so she sped up. "Why won't this jerk get off my ass?"

Next thing you know, there is the dreaded flashing lights. Oh shit. At the time, we were smoking a blunt, windows barely cracked. We quickly disposed of the blunt out the window and kept driving a little bit. We pulled off to the side of the road and after a second the officer came up to the window. You know it reeked like weed when we rolled the window down and I am pretty sure smoke came rolling out. I was so high that none of this even phased me. The officer asked for my friend's license, which she didn't have. He commented on how the car smelled like weed and mentioned how he saw us throw something out the window. "Oh, I am sorry officer; we have no idea what you are talking about." Yeah, we tried to play dumb.

The officer called for backup. In the meantime, he made us all get out of the car. As my friend in the front seat stepped out of the car, the officer mentioned something about him having weed all over his pants and shirt. He brushed it off and said, "No I don't." Next, we all come piling out of the back seat. One of my friends was drinking a tall boy. He was of age, but apparently it is frowned upon to have an open container in the car. The officer made him pour it out. Next, he sat us all on the curb. Did I mention it was January? It was freezing. I remember exactly what I was wearing. A pair of jeans, my white Hurley hoodie, and my black and green spitfire beanie. It was not very warm. He made us sit on that curb for thirty minutes or more so he could try to find the blunt roach we threw out the window. They never did find it. I was pissed they made us sit in the cold that long for something so small.

Next, they searched the car. They got into my bag and that is when the panic mode set in. I knew I had my pipe and some weed in there. Why didn't I leave it at the house? I don't know why I didn't think to leave it. Finally, they came over to the curb and asked who the bag belonged to. That is when I spoke up and said, "It belongs to me." And that is when it happened: my first time being arrested. They made me stand up and put my hands behind my back. Then, they slapped the cold metal handcuffs on my wrist.

They were tight and uncomfortable. They sent my friends on their way and they put me in the back of the cop car. While I was not happy about the situation, I was too high to really care that much.

The officers took me to the O'Fallon Police Station. They pulled into a weird spot and they took me into the jail. They booked me and processed me, all the while joking around with me. I did mention before that I was high, right? Well, they thought it was funny. Let's just put it this way: that day I smoked more blunts than I can count on one hand, plus I had drank some. They were joking about how bad I smelled like weed. They joked about how chilled and relaxed I was for being arrested for the first time. I was just kind of like whatever, might as well make light of a bad situation.

The booking and processing took about an hour. I was given a bail of four hundred dollars. I had gotten paid that day and I actually had quite a bit of cash on me. I had deposited the rest of my check. I had over half of it. I got a hold of Aaron to come and pick me up and bring the other part of the money. He arrived and I bonded myself out. We stopped at a bank on the way home so I could pay him back. We went back to his house and I spent the night there. All I could think about was how I was going to tell my parents about this one. I was going to have a court date and I figured they needed to know.

I remember driving in the car with my mom one day and telling her about it. She was not really shocked at all. She basically told me I was dumb and that she knew it would happen sooner or later. Well, okay then, thanks mom. But really she was right. I spent so much time thinking I was invincible while I made poor decisions. Of course, it was bound to happen eventually.

I called a lawyer and got him on my case. For this charge I never had to appear in court. I was able to get it dropped to a littering charge and I just had to pay a fine. It was just a little slap on the wrist. I should have learned from it and made better decisions, but that was not the case.

So let's fast forward just a couple months to March of 2007. I was hanging out with some friends and I went to pick up a quarter pound of weed. I was just dealing a little bit to make some extra cash and get pot. I was not a big time dealer and I tried to be careful about it. In reality, I was not smart about it. I always drove around with pot and my scales because I didn't really have any place to keep it. So I had gotten some weed and I had a couple people waiting on me to get it. I weighed out a couple of bags before we left so I could go drop it off. I had a friend with me who didn't even smoke pot. I was talking about how careful I am driving when I have stuff on me. I never wanted to give the cops any reason to pull me over. Literally, a minute after saying that, I saw cops lights flashing behind me. There is no way that is for me! I am going the speed limit and I have done nothing wrong. I was so nervous, I was literally shaking uncontrollably. I pulled over to the side of the road and my friend told me I needed to calm down. I tried to pull myself together before the cops came to the car, but I couldn't stop shaking. They came up to my window.

"Do you know why we pulled you over?"

"No, officer, I do not know," I said as my voice trembled. They told me I switched lanes without using my blinker. That was bullshit because I never even switched lanes. Somebody set me up. They wanted to search my car. I told them if they just pulled me over for not using my blinker, then they had no reason to search my car. Their reason was when they shined the flashlight in my car, they thought they had seen some weed or seeds on my floor. They said if they looked closer and it was what they thought, then they had reason to search my car. I call bullshit on this but whatever. They looked and it wasn't what they thought. I should be in the clear then right? Wrong. Then they told me they were going to go ahead and call in K9 units. What?!? All because I didn't use my blinker, they are going through all of this. Something here isn't matching up; somebody told on me.

I didn't believe they were really going to bring in K9 units. They kept telling me if I had something then I would be better to tell them before the dogs found it. I was standing my ground. I thought they were just bluffing. Next thing you know, here comes two more cops cars and here comes the dogs. The other officers get out and start talking to me and the cops that are on the scene. Before they got the dogs out, I confessed to having weed on me. They then searched my car and found the weed in my bag. I had a couple bags weighed out that I was on my way to sell. I had some scales, more weed, and some baggies. Well, this doesn't look good. There was no good explanation. They got me.

The police called a towing company and had my car towed. I guess I will have to tell my parents about this sooner or later. I begged and pleaded not to tow my car but they didn't listen. Once again they slapped the cold metal cuffs on my wrist. They put me in the back of the cop car. My friend had to come with us and get a ride from the police station. She was helping to keep me calm and make light of the situation. I am glad she didn't get into any trouble. The cops did lecture her, though, about choosing better friends. We pulled up to St. Peters Police Station where they took me in and booked me. My friend stayed out front and eventually found a ride home.

The police went through the whole booking process and asking me stupid questions. It took forever. I was able to pay money and get myself out. My car was towed so I had to call for a ride. I ended up having Brittany come and pick me up and went to a friend's house. I got wasted that night. Why not just drown your problems? It will all sink in tomorrow. I stayed out that night. Brittany gave me a ride to work in the morning. How am I going to tell my parents where my car is? I thought I would be able to get it out on my own without them even knowing. Since it was in their name, it wasn't going to work. I worked that day and went home. My parents asked where my car was. I told them I had gotten drunk so I got a ride and left it at a friend's house. After work that day, I tried to get my car back but I was turned down. It was a difficult process even trying to get it. I knew I would have to suck it up and tell my parents now.

I think I went through another day of lies about where my car was before I finally sucked it up and told my mom. After just getting arrested a couple months ago, she basically just told me I was stupid. She was right. I was stupid. She had to tell my dad and he had to go get my car with me. This was not a fun adventure at all. Apparently, whenever you let your car sit, it costs more money for each day it is there.

A little time had passed by and I thought I was in the clear. I had no court dates and nothing was filed. I had already spoken with my lawyer though. One day when I was at work, the sheriff's department showed up at my house. My mom was here when they came and I received a summons for court. So much for thinking I was lucky. This was it. I called my lawyer to let him know and was trying to get it taken care of. My charges were something to do with possession and sales. It was worse than my first arrest that I had. It could have been a felony charge.

I went to court and I got my sentence. I got the charges as two misdemeanors, one for possession and one for paraphernalia. I was put on two years unsupervised probation and I also had to take a class about drug abuse. It was an eight hour class on a Saturday. I was on misdemeanor probation so it was a little different. I also had to do community service which I was not happy about. Looking back at this, I am lucky it wasn't worse.

Well, there are my two arrest stories. I wish I could say they were my only two and that was it. Unfortunately, that is not the case. These ones were easier and not as bad. The last one is the worst of them all, my third strike. So much happened between these arrests and my last one that I must go through everything that leads up to it.

Chapter 9

2007- Leading Up To My Felonies

Here we are summertime, the best time of the year. It is festival season and lots of drugs, friends and good memories. I was nineteen, no school, just work and hanging out with friends. Nothing could possibly go wrong when you were having a good time. I drank every single day. My alcohol consumption had gotten out of control. I never went a day without Captain Morgan. I started out with buying a pint everyday but then I had to get more.

We would spend our summers going to festivals. I tried to make it to every single one that I could. I think this year in particular I had made it to them all. I would just tell my parents that I was going camping. It was a music festival, camping, good friends, and good music. I usually didn't shower and was dirty. Lots of dirty hippies and it was just a peaceful place. I don't know any other way to describe it, but a lot of good memories were made here. I've only briefly talked about it and so much happened and I went to so many, that there is no way for me to even put all of it together. If I tried to tell stories from every one I attended, that would be another book.

At this time, Linda and I were selling drugs to make extra cash. Our business was going pretty well at this point and we were always able to get extra work at festivals. We went to the first festival of the summer and met some new friends. They were mutual friends of people we knew but we hadn't met them yet. I met a boy who I connected with very well. His name was Evan and we had a great time. I believe he had a girlfriend at the time or was going through a break up. Nothing had happened at that time but later on we ended up dating. I will get to that shortly.

We had so much fun at our weekend getaways. That same weekend, we also met a guy named Jay. He was so awesome to hang out with. I had seen him at festivals before. He always stood out because he wore a Wal-Zones vest around. Linda and I hung out in his tent with him one night where I tried DMT for the first time. DMT is a powerful hallucinogenic. It was insane. I felt like I was a cartoon character and I also thought my hair turned into yarn. I kept feeling my hair and having everyone feel it because it turned to yarn. I thought it was all falling out. It was such an intense high and an insane trip. The good thing is that it doesn't last long. I couldn't imagine feeling that messed up for hours. It was way more intense than mushrooms or acid. Jay fell asleep and we left his tent. We wandered around where I did more and more drugs. I stayed up all night and just listened to music, high as a kite.

The next day we wandered around and went to find our friends. Evan had left his hat in the grass where we laid, so I made sure to go find him to give it back. He was excited that I brought it to him because he thought he lost it. Then, I made sure I went to find Jay so I could give him my number. I found him and talked to him for a little while. Then, we ended up heading home. I hated coming home. It was always miserable. My whole body would ache and my brain was fried. The amount of drugs I would consume in one weekend was just ridiculous. I will say it again, how am I even still alive today? It usually took me a little while to recover from the weekend. I am not sure how I even functioned when I got back home. I would barely sleep through the weekend. Every time I came home, the first thing I would do was eat, take a shower and then I would sleep as long as I possibly could.

It was back to reality. I was back to my parent's house and back to work at King Burger. When I got back home, I talked to Jay on the phone almost every day. We would talk forever about

49

everything. A few days later, I called him and he didn't return my call. I figured he was busy and he would just call me back. I tried again later that evening and still nothing. Just a couple days later, I got a call from his dad and a message saying that he had passed away. Even though we had just met, we had become extremely close. I was devastated. Linda and I went out to his funeral. It was pretty tough. I just couldn't believe it happened, just like that.

At this time in my life, my drinking was getting pretty bad. I would drink every single day. I started by getting pints of Captain every night. I then began getting fifths and eventually I would get a handle every day. That is about a half-gallon of alcohol. I never went a day without alcohol and I am pretty sure that the majority of my money went to support my drinking habits. I spent about one hundred and fifty dollars a week on drinking. I was also eating a lot of acid and ecstasy because I was selling it at the time. We were hanging out at our friend Cory and Evan's house all the time. Linda started dating Cory and I eventually started dating Evan. I would sleep over there a lot. I usually got too drunk to drive home anyway. The majority of the time I would end up black out drunk. And I truly mean blacked out because there are so many things I just do not remember. People would tell me stories the next day and I would have zero recollection. I would get into fights with people. Not usually real fights, I just liked to wrestle with people when I was drunk.

Cory and Evan's house is where I met my friend Brian, but we referred to him as "Brain". The funny thing is that legally that is what his name was because they misspelled it on his birth certificate. I will never forget the first time I hung out with him one on one. I think for once I was actually sober or I had only had a few drinks. I can't remember why I was the sober one because that was rare. I drove him up to the gas station to buy more alcohol. He asked me why I was so sad. I looked at him and asked what he meant. He told me he could read people and see their emotions. I looked at him and he just told me exactly how I felt and read me like a book. It was crazy and from that day forward we became best friends. I talked to him about everything and he never judged me. It pains me to write about this since he is no longer with us today. I will never forget him and I still always wish I could just call him up and talk to him, just to hear his voice at least one more time.

This was just an absolute crazy time in my life. I was partying hard. I had a pretty set schedule at work of Monday-Friday from 8a.m. until 4p.m. I am surprised I made it work every day. I would occasionally over sleep or end up drunk and passed out at some random place. I think that only happened once and, well, I was throwing up at work that day. I made it to work, but I was about an hour late. That was a bad day. I would occasionally work weekends.

I will never forget one of my craziest weekends ever. I think when I try to explain it now it might not seem as crazy or it may even sound worse. It started on a Friday night. Linda and I had decided to eat some acid. We were hanging out at Cory and Evan's house that night. We were still selling drugs at that point, too. We went and sold some drugs to one of her friends or a friend of a friend. I can't exactly remember. We were tripping and I am not sure what the person was talking about, but I remember him talking about killing someone. We freaked out and left. After that, we had to go to drop stuff off to another person. I didn't really want to go there. I wanted to go back to relax and enjoy our trip. The guy offered me a line of cocaine if I went to drop it off to him. I couldn't pass up an offer for some free drugs. We got there and our acid was kicking in even more. I snorted a huge line of coke. We hung out there for just a little bit and him and his brother were getting into a fight. It was a big mess and we snuck out of there as quickly as we could.

Finally, we made it back to Evan's house. We could relax and enjoy our drugs. The coke and acid didn't mix well and for a little bit I was freaking out. I literally could feel my heart pounding up against my chest. When I looked in the mirror, I could watch my heart beating. I was freaking out. I just had to keep taking deep breaths to try to calm myself down. It eventually got better and I was just tripping. That night, we sat around and played Monopoly. It was fun except I couldn't concentrate or figure out how to play. I had to have people help me count my money. We played until about two or three in the morning. Linda's parents were out of town and we were going to stay at her house. We left there and drove to her house and we were still tripping. We get to her house and realized her dog was sick. He didn't look good and there was throw up all around the house. We freaked out and found an emergency animal clinic that was open twenty four hours. We had to drive there as quickly as we could and ran in with her dog. It was insane and I am sure we looked messed up because, well, we were. Her dog had swallowed something and had to have it removed. I believe it was a sharp object like a needle. The vets said it could have been there for a long time but just began to cause problems.

We left and went back to her house. I tried to get some sleep but it just was not happening. The next day, I went home and tried to rest. I never did fall asleep or if I did it was not a long time. I ran around and did some errands. I felt bad for Linda with her dog so I remember delivering her one of her favorite pizzas.

Later that evening, we went back to Cory and Evan's house. Everyone wanted to eat ecstasy that night. I didn't know if my mind and body could handle it. I still hadn't recovered from eating acid the night before. I was beyond exhausted and I really wanted to get some sleep that night. I had to work early the next day so I wanted to make sure I got enough sleep. I said I wasn't going to take any. Of course, I was talked into it. It was never hard to talk me into it. I somehow was a functioning addict. I would always get so messed up, never sleep and I was always able to work. Everyone said I would be fine but I decided I would just call into work. I even wrote myself a note and set an alarm to make sure I called into work at the right time. So I snorted some ecstasy. I didn't do a whole lot but it was just enough. I drank with it as well. I stayed up all night and come morning time I made that phone call to my work. I was never good at calling off and I didn't do it much. It didn't go well and because they didn't have enough people, I had to go into work anyway.

That day at work was miserable. I was able to push through but I was mentally and physically exhausted. Two nights of drugs and no sleep at all. I had a hard time making it through that day and I was so excited when I got off work. I got to the point I was so overly exhausted that I was actually more awake. I wanted to go home and sleep but I just couldn't. I went and hung out with some friends for a little bit. I drank a little and I smoked some pot. I got some Xanax and then I went home, took that and I went to bed. That was the most amount of hours I think I have ever been awake consecutively. I forget what the exact amount of hours was, I think by the time I went to sleep I had been awake for sixty hours. It took a little while to recover from that.

That is pretty much how my summer went. I did the same things all the time. I was still on that two year probation from my prior arrests but I didn't see my probation officer much. I was still selling drugs and I loved the adrenaline from it. I had also started snorting heroin a little bit at this time. Cory and I started doing it and we promised it would just be an every once in awhile type of thing. We agreed we wouldn't make a habit out of it and we didn't tell anyone. Evan would've flipped shit if he knew; it was pretty much just me and a select few who were doing it. We had to hide it from everyone else. We would sit there all relaxed and just nodding out slightly. I am not sure how we even kept it a secret. I would get off work, go over there, and Cory would have it in the bathroom for me. I would run in there and snort it. It started out just every once in awhile. Then it would be a few times a week. It just gradually began happening more frequently. Evan found out and he was not happy with any of us. He was especially not happy with me since I was his girlfriend and I was hiding it, knowing that he wouldn't like it. I thought it was going to ruin our relationship. We eventually talked him into trying it and, of course, he liked it. I feel guilty; we should've never had him do it. It was for selfish reasons because I wanted to keep getting high. It made it a lot easier when we no longer had to hide it. It is one of those drugs you should just never try. You will like it and you can't just do it every once in awhile. You will become addicted. It will eventually take over your whole life and control you.

I don't even know exactly how the heroin addiction began. We were snorting heroin a lot and that's what we spent all of our time doing. The people who didn't do it didn't care to hang out with us as much. I would let people borrow my car to go get it while I was at work. I loved snorting heroin and I didn't feel like I was that bad. I mean I didn't get "dope" sick, at least not yet anyway or not horrible. Also, I worked to support my habit. I wasn't stealing or anything. Plus, we were just snorting it. It is not like we were using needles, so we weren't that bad, right? This was just the beginning.

Chapter 10

The Big Arrest

It was an October day and I was working a double. When I got off work, I had some deals to make. This kid I knew wanted some acid and I told him I would meet him after work. Thinking about it now, the text messages did seem weird. I mean I sold to him a lot but the way he kept asking and his persistence seemed unusual. Of course, at the time I thought nothing of it. I just had money on my mind. Little did I know, the drug task force had been staked outside my work and watched me the whole day. I didn't even think of it until they mentioned it later but they had even come in and ate at my work. I recognized them from earlier that day.

I finally got off work around seven or eight. I went to pick up Linda to go with me to make the deal. We were in this together. On the way there, we were smoking a bowl of pot and just listening to music. We were just laughing and having a good time. We had no idea what was going to happen next. We pulled up the kid's house to sell him the drugs. I parked the car and Linda was on the passenger's side cutting the acid. Next thing you know, two cars came flying at us with their brights on. One was an SUV and the other was a truck. They flew at my car so fast that I thought they were going to hit me. One parked in front and the other parked behind me to sandwich me in. We looked at each other and barely had time to speak before we were being thrown on the ground. They yelled at us and were telling us we were under arrest. I was in complete and total shock.

There were four of them, all men. They pulled us out of the car, two on each side. They were huge and didn't treat us like young girls. No, they didn't care how rough they were. They thought I was resisting because I was caught on my seatbelt when they tried to throw me on the ground. One stayed with each of us while the others tore my car apart. They separated us and put both of us in hand cuffs. There they were again, those cold metal cuffs. They put Linda in one car and me in the other car. I was terrified. I broke down in tears. I just didn't know what to do. I had way too much drugs to incriminate me and I had already been in trouble. What was I going to do? What were my parents going to say? I was dead.

As they spoke to me, the drug task force asked questions like, "How can you live like this? You are not going to get anywhere living this way." It was basically lectures that I was headed down the wrong path. As if I hadn't heard that one before. In my car, I had over an ounce of weed with a couple of bags weighed out. I also had twenty four hits of acid, which is what I was most worried about. There was no getting out of this one. They kept yelling at me in my face and I was just crying. I know they were trying to place fear in me. I remember I would cry and agreed with them that I was messing my life up. I knew I needed help. I also remember getting pissed off at them and getting an attitude because they just ruined my night. It was a little back and forth.

They took us down to the O'Fallon Police Station. Here we go again, another arrest. They brought us into an interview room, one at a time. They kept asking questions but I absolutely refused to give them any information. I said that I didn't get anything from around here that I had brought it back from my camping trip. They wanted more information. I told them I didn't get it from anyone local. Finally, I made up some names. My ticket out that night was letting them search my house. I was young and didn't know much about the law. They had no right coming into my house. It got me a free card for the night, which meant I was in the clear, right? Haha! Far from it!

They drove me to my house and came into my room. My parents were home sleeping while all of this was going on. I knew I didn't have anything at my house which is why I didn't care that they came in. I was just hoping they would be quiet and hurry up. That would've been horrible if my parents had gotten up. I couldn't even imagine having that happen. Not that it would really matter because they would eventually find out anyway.

Finally, I got back to my car and the task force just dropped me off. I was in shock and I didn't know what to do. I kept thinking, is this a test? They are tricking me. I feel like they are playing a joke on me and they are going to pull me over as soon as I drive. I was supposed to contact them the next day, the guy gave me a fake name and his cell phone number. I was so confused. I sat in my car and I looked at the mess they made tearing it apart. Of course they were not cleaning that up. I grabbed my phone and I realized the number of missed calls that I had. We were going to Cory and Evan's after we made our transaction. They were worried and wondering where we were. I opened up my center council and I found my pipe and my personal weed sitting right where I left it. How did they miss it? Or were they just being nice and left it for me? I don't think it would've mattered even if they did find it. I had enough stuff to get me into trouble. I was also glad when I saw they didn't take my envelope filled with money.

I called Evan to let him know what happened. I forget if I picked Linda up or if she was with me, but we went over to our boyfriend's house. We told them everything that happened. It was crazy. I was in so much shock and I was scared to death. I called off work for the next day and I got hammered drunk. I just tried to forget about it.

The next day I called my lawyer. The drug task force guys told me to call them and that I didn't need to call my lawyer or my probation officer. They said if I just worked with them I would get out of trouble. Of course, I said I would call them and that I would help them out. Instead, I called my lawyer and told him everything. He said, "Whatever you do don't call those scumbags back." I also called my probation officer to tell her. I wasn't officially revoked yet, but I knew I was pretty much going to be done with that probation. I had only been on it for a few months or so. When I spoke to her she talked about how mad she would be if someone was selling drugs to her kids. She had kids about the same age as the person I was selling to that night. I kind of understood her point but I really didn't care. Teenagers will make their own decisions. After speaking to her that day, I just didn't go back to her.

I met with my lawyer and I told him everything that happened. He mentioned how they had no right to come into my house the way they did. He said I should've never let them. I guess I didn't think it really mattered since I knew I didn't have anything. I think they thought they would find the mother load of drugs at my house. We talked about our plan of action and what would happen. We couldn't do anything until my charges popped up. I had to always check case net to look for when they popped up. I thought I was in the clear since I heard nothing from the task force. I knew I wasn't that lucky but I thought maybe they did something wrong. Maybe they couldn't charge me because they messed up on my arrest. Unfortunately, that wasn't the case.

After this, I just went on about my life. I continued to do what I always did, work and party. I would work all day and get drunk and high all night. Absolutely nothing changed. I guess it didn't scare me enough. The heroin was beginning to get worse, too. It was becoming more frequent now that we didn't have to hide it from Evan. He wanted to do it too which made it easier. I still didn't think I was an addict and I still thought I was invincible. Even after I got caught three times, I still thought I was invincible. No, really I was just stupid.

Chapter 11

They Got Me

Several months after my arrests nothing had happened. I still thought the drug task force did something wrong and maybe they couldn't get me for it. I thought I was one hundred percent in the clear. I can't remember if I had told my parents yet or not. I think they may have known something but not the full extent of it. My parents obviously knew I was headed down the wrong path. They didn't know exactly what all I was up to but they knew it was nothing good. No matter how hard they tried to help me and stop me, they couldn't. I completely shut them out unless I needed their help. I was a manipulator and they were unknowingly my enablers.

It was a typical day at work. It was about nine in the morning and I had just finished cleaning up the parking lot at King Burger. I was in the back of the store and I was about to begin on dishes. I looked over where you could see in the dining room. As I did, I saw two guys both at least six foot five or more. They had on their SWAT team vests and made my manager look like an ant next to them. I made direct eye contact with them and they gave me the finger wave of come here now. For a split second I thought about running, but I knew it wouldn't do me any good. My heart sank into my stomach and I felt nauseous. This was it. They were up there talking to my manager Julie as I headed up front. They basically said, "You know what you've done. You didn't think you could possibly get away with this, did you?" Of course, I did; I thought I was invincible. No, I didn't actually say that out loud, but it is the thought that crossed my mind. In all reality, I knew it would eventually catch up to me. I mean I had twenty four hits of acid. They kind of make a big deal about that kind of stuff.

I felt horrible leaving work that day. I didn't want to leave them short-handed, but I obviously had no choice. I asked them if I could go grab my jacket and, of course, one of them had to follow me. They wanted to make sure I wasn't going to dart out the back door. The thought remained in the back of my mind but I knew it'd be stupid to run. I would get caught and it would make things worse. As he followed me back to get my jacket I said, "You know, you really don't have to follow me. I am just getting my jacket."

I was being a smart ass and my mouth was only getting me into more trouble. I was just angry that they came to my work to pick me up. I mean was that really necessary? I walked up front and as I clocked out I began to cry. I can't explain the emotions. It was a lot of anger and a lot of me just being terrified. I just didn't want to go to jail and this was way more serious than my other charges. One of the officers made a smart ass remark about me crying so I flipped him off and I mumbled "fuck you" under my breath which was probably not the brightest idea. My manager just looked at me in disbelief and shook her head like "did you really just do that?" The officer laughed about it and with his cocky little attitude said, "Oh you just wait, we are going to have fun."

They hand cuffed me in front of all the people I work with. I cried a little bit more as they walked me out of the dining room in front of everyone and took me to their big black truck. They put me in the back and I had a million thoughts running through my head. Here we go. They began driving and they wanted to talk to me like we were best friends. I just kept my mouth shut and didn't give them the time of day. They asked me about my jobs, school, and any kind of small talk they could come up with. They were trying to reel me in, but I wasn't biting their bait.

61

The officer turned back to me and said, "Alright, you have one last chance. Work for us and all of this will go away. None of this will be on your record. You just have to make one phone call and set one drug deal. Then you are free and it is like none of this ever happened."

I laughed slightly. Did they really think I was that stupid? I replied, "So that is all I have to do and I won't be in any trouble at all? And what if I don't? What happens if I refuse to do that?"

"Yes, one call and it all will go away. If you do not, well, that is up to the judge and it's really not looking very good for you."

With my shit don't stink attitude I replied, "I will take my chances. I would never help you out."

They didn't like my answer but there was nothing they could do to change it. I refused to help them. They took me to St. Charles County jail. They gave me one last chance but I gave them the same answer.

I was taken up to booking and I was given a $50,000 bond. At ten percent I needed five thousand dollars in cash to get out. Where am I going to come up with that kind of money and how the hell am I going to get out of here? I was hand cuffed to the bench. The correctional officers began my booking and processing, which I must say they take their sweet time with. I kept begging to make a phone call. They didn't allow me to for awhile. I was getting angry and the time was going so slow it felt like it was at a stand-still. There was no way to get comfortable when you are handcuffed to a bench and the officers were being assholes. After awhile, the same two officers came walking in with Linda. They also went to pick her up from work. I tried talking to her, but she was feeling the same way as I was. She was scared and we were both afraid of our parents' reaction.

I was finally able to make a phone call and I called my mom. Luckily, my manager Julie had already called them so they knew. It helped to get the process started a little quicker, but they still took their time. Both of my parents left work early that day and spent their day talking to lawyers and getting the cash for my bail. From the time I began working, my dad always made me put twenty percent of every paycheck into savings. I also had put a lot of money in there from my graduation. So, luckily, I had enough money in my savings to pay my bail. The money would end up going towards my lawyer fees after posting bail.

The hours were passing by. I watched people come and go. Linda's parents even came to get her before I got out. I remained hand cuffed to that bench becoming more and more angry. It had been about five hours when I called my parents yelling at them to hurry the hell up. They said they were trying. I should've been grateful that they were even coming to get me. They could've left me and that would have been the smart thing to do. I stayed hand cuffed to that bench for a total of about six or seven hours that day. I was so excited when I finally got out. I just had to appear in court, time to start the process. My parents drove me home. Talk about an awkward car ride.

As soon as we got home, I ran up to shower and got ready to go out. I was ready to party after all of that. The weather was supposed to get bad that night and my parents didn't really want me going out. It didn't matter. I was going anyways. I went over to my friend Mike's house. He lived down the street. We drank a couple bottles of Jim Beam and snorted some heroin. I got out of my mind that night which was exactly what I wanted to do. I was angry after my day and being in a different state of mind was my release.

The next day I felt like shit and it was time to face reality now. It hadn't all settled in yet but I knew some bad things were coming my way. Now it is time for me to put my big girl pants on and deal with it. I wasn't sure what was going to happen next. I honestly didn't really want to even think about it. Any time I did think about it, it just made me feel sick.

Chapter 12

2008- The Year of Court Dates

It was back to my daily grind. I was doing the same things as usual. I was working, drinking and getting high. I was still with Evan and I would spend my free time over there. I was there a lot. We spent that summer going to festivals again. I didn't go to as many this year. I was trying to save money for my court and lawyer costs, but I couldn't seem to save money. It all went to drugs.

I was trying to lay low and be careful considering I already knew I was in trouble. I wasn't going to probation and I didn't have to worry about any drug tests for that. I had a lot of court dates. My lawyer would go to most of my court dates and they would be continued. I only had to appear for some. It seemed like it was such a long and drawn out process.

At some point in here, I even got a second job. I started delivering pizzas for a local pizzeria. It was just some extra cash but to me that meant extra money for drugs. I was afraid trying to get a job since I had felonies. They did a background check but I passed since I have not actually been convicted yet. My life continued to spiral downhill. Even though I tried to stay clean and stay out of trouble, I couldn't stop. It was getting worse.

My actual charges ended up being three class B felonies for sales and distribution of a controlled substance. I was mad that the system tacked on three, especially after reading the report to find out what the third one was. I had a jar that had dust from ecstasy in it. They charged me another distribution charge for that even though I didn't have any on me. No matter what, I was screwed.

I had to appear in court one day for my sentencing. This was it. This was the final day. I walked into court that day and I was dressed nice. At least, for me I was dressed the best I could. I was wearing a black skirt, a white V-neck shirt, and black open toe dress shoes. I was terrified. My parents were there with me that day. I had to stand in front of the judge. The judge seemed nice and he seemed fair but the prosecuting attorney was not nice at all. It was the moment of truth. I sat up on the stand and was scared. I knew this was the moment of truth. I can't remember exactly how it went down. I just know I was sentenced to one hundred and twenty days in the women's correctional facility for a treatment program. I had an eight year back up and I was put on five years of SES probation. I didn't even know what all that meant at the time but it means I am convicted. It is permanently on my record, although I am hopeful that I can change that one day. I wasn't going to have to go to jail that day. I could've turned myself in at a later date. I was given certain stipulations to be free and one of them was I had to go get a drug test. I was mad and refused to do so. Then, they put me in hand cuffs and took me from the court room that day.

It was my first time actually having to stay in jail. I was stupid for letting my attitude put me there that day. The officers took me over straight from court. I had to dress out into oranges for the first time. They made me take off all my clothes. I had to squat and cough in front of the officer before I changed out. I had to put on nasty looking granny panties. The oranges were big and baggy and the shoes were ridiculous. I couldn't believe I had to go through this. They took me down to a pod. I was terrified. I didn't know what to do or where to go. I was upset and crying. I was sitting in the day room and started talking to some people. This one girl was talking to me and she helped me out a lot. She explained everything to me and helped me to get stamps and envelopes to write to my parents.

I was immediately calling my lawyer to help me to get out. It was a Friday when I went in so it was hard to get a hold of him. I had to wait until Monday to really get anything to happen. That was the longest weekend ever. I got a hold of my parents to put money on my books so I could get essentials from commissary. I didn't know how long I was going to be there. The beds were uncomfortable and the food was disgusting. There was nothing to do. I read a lot of books while I was in there and I wrote a lot, too. After getting a hold of my lawyer, I was able to set up a court date. I had to wait but I was able to get back in front of the judge. I was able to get out of jail. I agreed to take the drug test which I had to go do on my own. I just had to come back to turn myself in to begin my actual prison sentence. I had spent about two weeks in jail that first time. It felt like forever and I was excited to go home.

I never did get that drug test. I was told I had to turn myself in to St. Charles County jail on January 5. This gave me a couple months to get everything in order and I was able to enjoy my holidays. In other words, it just gave me more time to get high. I was supposed to be saving up money so I would have money for when I went to prison. Instead, I spent all of my money on drugs and I had to rely on my parents' help when I was in prison. I enjoyed my last few months of freedom before I went away.

Chapter 13

My Four Month Prison Journey

It was January 5, 2009, when I had to turn myself in. My parents and Evan dropped me off at St. Charles County jail and from there I would be transported to Vandalia, MO where the women's correctional facility was located. It was a little over an hour drive from St. Charles. I was glad I was able to wait until after the holidays. I didn't want to leave my boyfriend and be away from him for that long. It was hard to turn myself in that day. Even though I knew it was coming, it didn't make it any easier. I would sit in the county jail until I was transported, but the time there didn't count towards my prison sentence. Luckily, I was only there for two days when they woke me up early and told me to bunk n junk. That's what they call it when you get to pack up all of your belongings and leave. I was nervous and excited. I knew this meant my time was beginning. I packed up all of my stuff, put on my oranges and slipped on my shoes. I met the officer at the sliding doors.

The correctional officers took me up to holding where I had to sit and wait. Of course, I was hand cuffed to that bench again. It was early so not too much excitement was going on there. There were a few guys on the other side and they act like they haven't seen a female in years, even though they've probably only been there for twenty four hours! I had to wait for the other girl who was being transported to prison with me. Finally, she showed up and it was time to get ready and go. They put the shackles on us. We were put in ankle cuffs and hand cuffs. Ugh, I was really getting sick of these damn things! Since it was only me and one other person, we were transported in the back of a cop car. Sometimes they would take big groups and they pile them all into a van. I felt lucky with it being only me and one other person. Especially with what we went through when we got there!

It was a long, boring drive. The person with me fell asleep and was snoring. I couldn't sleep, not even the thought of it sounded fun. I don't know if "scared" is the right word, but I definitely had a lot of emotions going through me as we made that drive. I kept thinking of how I am only twenty years old and here I go to prison. What will it be like? I am young and I am vulnerable. Will they eat me alive? What if people steal my belongings? There were so many thoughts running through my head. I just didn't know what to expect.

Finally, after what felt like the longest drive ever, we arrived. We pulled up and I thought, this is what prison looks like! We are in the middle of nowhere and it looked like a bunch of big red barns, interesting. We got out of the car and we were escorted in for processing. The officer dropped us off and said good luck as she headed back to St. Charles. My stomach sank as it began to set in: this is it, and here I am in prison.

It all started from there. First, the correctional officers asked a thousand questions about literally everything. Then, they stripped me of my dignity. I have always been a modest person, I don't like changing clothes in front of anyone but they took that away from me. I had to go into a cold, scary room. It was me and the person I had ridden down with and two correctional officers. "Alright, I need you to take off all of your clothes, squat and cough, and spread your butt cheeks." What?!? They have got to be joking with me right now! They don't really expect me to do that. But they did and I had to. So here I go, feeling helpless and disgusted. I wanted to hide. Next, I was able to put my clothes back on, for a little bit anyways. I was so glad that was over, but it was not the end. It was only the beginning.

Next on the list was the shower with lice shampoo and getting dressed out into our state grays. Once again, me and the girl I was with had to strip down. This time it was in front of the people who run the clothing section of the prison, which happens to be inmates. There were three of them and they could see the fear in us. We each had our own shower where we had to use lice shampoo and freezing cold water. The towel they gave us was literally a hand towel. As I came out of the shower to get my clothes, I tried my best to cover my naked body with that little towel, but it just wasn't big enough. It kept falling. It was time to try on our outfits. I got some khaki, some grays, shirts and pants. Oh, and don't forget about the black witch boots. They really expect me to wear this outfit for the next four months? Oh my.

We finished all of our processing. We got our photos taken for our prison IDs and received our DOC numbers. We got our bag of stuff, stocked full of our clothes, blankets, etc. It was everything I had to my name at that time. Then we had to sit and wait. There was a bus load of people from another county that had come in and we had to wait for them to finish up their processing. I was getting nervous to actually go into the prison and meet the other inmates. As terrified as I was, I didn't want to let it show.

It was time to go. We threw our bags over our shoulders and took the march of shame. We were put into receiving and orientation (R&O) which is where everyone starts their sentence. You get a mix of everyone in there. We were given our room assignments and in we walked. Everyone stops what they're doing and stares at the fresh meat walking in. I ignored the stares and went directly into my room. I was thankful I had a bunk in a room.

Some people's bunks were out in the dayroom. As a person who likes privacy, I couldn't have been happier to be in a room.

Now from here things get a little blurry. I will try to remember as many details as I can, but it was so long ago and a lot happened at this time. I can't remember my first set of roommates and I can't remember the first person who came to talk to me. I do remember that I did always get pretty lucky with bunkies and I do remember people being helpful. I was given the 411 on how things work. I was also scared of a lot of the people I saw. You never know what each person is in there for or what their story is.

So day one, here I am in prison, only 119 days more to go. You couldn't do anything and each day was the exact same. We had to wake up at 4:30 A.M. to go to breakfast. After that we had counts. That was when we had to sit in our rooms and must be sitting up in our bunks and facing the door. We would be there for an hour or more sometimes. The officers would come around and make sure all the females in the prison were accounted for. Basically, to make sure nobody had escaped, I guess. Then we just hung out in the day room. There was one television and however many inmates, in other words, nobody ever always agreed. We had tables to sit at and played board/card games, colored, wrote letters, etc. We would go to lunch in a single file line and come back in a single file line. The food was absolutely repulsive, but you get used to it. You really don't have any other choice. We had more counts and we had shower times. Then, it was dinner time and again just sit and do nothing. We'd drink lots of keefe coffee. You can only get it in jail and we referred to it as jailhouse crack. We weren't allowed to sleep during the day or anything which totally sucked. The days were extremely long. I would always try to sneak in naps at count time. I just had to be super sneaky. You get in big trouble for sleeping during count time.

I forgot the exact number of days I was in R&O but I want to say it was about three weeks. Oh, and I forgot to mention the lice outbreaks. Those were scary. A few people had to get their heads shaved. I am pretty sure I would have freaked out if that happened to me. As soon as someone got lice, we would all be braiding our hair and greasing it up. It sounds crazy, but nobody wanted to get lice so we took precautions.

So after about three weeks, I was moved into the treatment wing. I was not ready for it and I just remember crying my eyes out the first day. I didn't want to be there but really it was my fault. The treatment had a lot of rules. It was extremely overwhelming. The first day was just too much for me. I wanted to just sign out and take my time. I knew that meant a lot of time, though, so I had to just suck it up.

We had to wake up at the same time each day for counts and breakfast. We had a set schedule with breaks and different groups all day long. It was the busiest days which sucked, but at the same time it was good because the days went by fast. We had all kinds of different groups led by counselors or other inmates. It was basically a behavior modification program. We worked a twelve step program and had NA/AA groups. I don't even remember what else we did. I just know our days were packed full.

The best part about being moved to treatment was we were able to smoke cigarettes. We had scheduled smoke breaks where we stood outside in a line. They were always checking to make sure we had receipts for our cigarettes and that nobody else gave you one. I don't know why, but I thought it was pretty stupid. You're not allowed to share stuff in there, but everyone always did. I got caught not having a receipt for mascara and got written up for it. It was so dumb.

One good thing was we were able to go to the rec center. While there I started getting into working out. It made me feel good and it felt like a good thing for my recovery at the time. I was able to not gain any weight while I was in prison. Most people easily gain fifteen or more pounds by eating the food and being sedentary. I mean, our meals were not the greatest. Each meal had at least two pieces of bread. We were also able to get visits. The worst part about visits was we had to dress out, which meant going through the stripping naked in front of the officers, squat, cough, and spread your cheeks. It was so gross. I only had one visit. I didn't want to go through that again. I was excited when my parents came to visit, but it was also weird having them see me in that situation.

I thought I had recovery all figured out. I thought I was going to get out and everything would be easy. I had no idea what I was getting myself into. I didn't realize how much work you need to put into it and I was still young. It was technically my first time in treatment. I didn't really count the outpatient my parents forced me to do. I guess I had yet to fully accept the fact I was an addict. I still thought I was just a normal teenager having fun. I thought I could stop doing drugs if I wanted to, I didn't think I was addicted. Also, I justified by the fact I was only snorting heroin at that time and not shooting it. There were people way worse than me. I wasn't even twenty one yet and I was turning twenty one a month after getting out of prison. I wondered how that was going to work for me. I could just drink and that would be okay, right?

The whole time I was in prison, I was angry knowing my friends and boyfriend were out still getting high. I thought it wasn't fair that they could get high. I knew I wouldn't be able to get high when I got out. A part of me still wanted to get high, but the other part said no you will stay clean, you do not want to come back to prison. I had an eight year back up and because of my felonies I would have to serve a higher percentage. I didn't want to do that. So that seemed like a good enough reason to stay clean. At least that is what you would think.

Finally, it was my day to be set free. It was only four months but it still seemed like forever. My parents were coming to pick me up. I couldn't wait to put on regular clothes and be on the other side of that gate. I was so excited to eat regular food and smoke Camels instead of cheap and nasty cigarettes. I forget what my first meal was but I know I ate a lot! I remember making my parents stop at the gas station so I could get cigarettes on my way home. I was so happy just looking around and looking at the world as we drove home. I was excited to go see my friends and my boyfriend. I was also nervous because I knew they were all still getting high. I knew I couldn't, though, and I wanted to stay clean. I realized just because my life changed and was put on hold doesn't mean my friends lives changed. Their life went on as usual without me.

On the way home I had to go meet my probation officer. I was nervous because I didn't want someone mean barking orders at me. I came to realize that I didn't have much respect for authority or anyone who thought they had power over me. Just as I suspected, my probation officer was not nice. She told me exactly how it was going to be and that I would follow the rules and everything she said. She tried to put the fear in me. I would report when I was supposed to report and follow the other guidelines. One of my stipulations was to complete an outpatient treatment program. I was not happy about that one. I just spent four months doing treatment in prison; why did I need to continue? In the beginning, I had to meet with her every two weeks. It would eventually go down to once a month with good behaviors. I was going to try my best to not get into any trouble or find my ways to beat the system. I did not want to go back to prison.

Chapter 14

Life After Prison

I was so excited to be out of prison and carry on with my life. It took a little bit of time to get used to being back to reality. I wasn't working at first and I wasn't really sure what I was planning to do yet. I still had my job at King Burger and I was able to go back to the pizzeria as well. I was trying to get settled back into my routine and trying to learn a new way of life. I enrolled into an outpatient treatment. I forget how long after getting out that I started, but I know there was a little bit of time in between.

I was hanging out with my old friends again. They smoked pot in front of me, but were courteous enough to not do heroin in front of me. I struggled to stay strong not to smoke pot, I don't think I could have said no to heroin right in front of my face. I still watched them all sit there and high on heroin just nodding out. It wasn't easy, but I was putting myself in that situation. I should've known better. I even ended up breaking up with my boyfriend shortly after getting out of prison. I had a lot of time to think while I was in prison and I really thought it'd be best for my recovery. I really needed to work on myself. I thought I was doing the right thing for my recovery and I knew I had to quit hanging out with my old friends so much. My relationship with Evan was by far the most stable relationship I ever had. I feel bad that I broke up with him thinking it would help me stay clean. In the end, he was the one who got clean and my life spiraled downhill. He was a great guy and was super nice and caring.

I started back to work at both of my jobs. I had my second meeting with my probation officer and went down to once a month. At some point, I began my outpatient program. I am trying to remember exactly when and how that began. That started out as three days a week and would go down to twice a week. So it seems as if everything is falling into place and going perfect, right? Wrong. I think it was about two weeks after I got out that I decided to snort heroin. It would just be a onetime thing, that's what I told myself. I know that's never the case though. I thought I was so cool using my prison idea to put my line together. Wow, I am stupid. It didn't take much to get high, I mean I was clean for almost five months. I just knew that heroin would get out of my system quick but if I smoked pot it would stay in my system.

So many changes were going on in my life. It was overwhelming. I started my outpatient classes, broke up with my boyfriend, adjusting to being back to reality, and on top of it all, I had my twenty first birth day. It's not good to turn twenty one a month after getting out of prison when you are trying to do the right thing. Of course I went out on my birthday and I got wasted. I don't think I did any drugs that I know of, just alcohol and lots of it. I went to a bar with a handful of friends. I was drinking a lot and of course people were buying me shots. Next thing you know, I am wasted. I don't think I got too out of control though, just having fun and being a happy drunk. My friends took me home and dropped me off at my house. I was beyond wasted and I ended up falling asleep on my front porch for a while before I actually made it up to my bed! I woke up feeling alright though, not too hungover.

I finally went down to twice a week at my outpatient classes and my heroin addiction was coming back in full swing. I guess it wasn't too bad because I was trying to time it right to make sure I would be clean if I had to take a drug test. This worked for a while but not for too long. I wanted to be able to do it more. Then I would just hope I wouldn't get dropped. My first dirty drop (failed drug test) I used the excuse that it was Vicodin. I said it was left over

77

from when I broke my tailbone. I guess you're wondering how I broke my tailbone, funny story actually. I was at the Offsets with some friends and I was pretty much blackout drunk. The Offsets is a quarry of water with cliffs to jump off of. I am not sure if I broke it hitting the water when jumping off a cliff or if it was when I was trying to stand up straight and I totally wiped out and fell on my ass. Either way, I know I did a bunch of heroin to ease the pain, which didn't work. Oh, and I ended up going to the ER to get x-rays and Vicodin. After running out of Vicodin, I went back and manipulated them into giving me another script. Plus, I did more heroin on top of that. That was not a good idea while being in rehab. My first dirty drop I had a consultation and just got a slap on the wrist. I knew I had to get my addiction under control. I knew it was time to fake it until I make it.

I tried to fake it. My addiction only got worse. At some point in here, I used a needle for the first time. Everything went downhill after that, bad. I am going to try describing it the best I can without glorifying it or making myself nauseous. My friends were doing it and, well, I wanted to also. I never did like needles much and I was terrified. It looked like fun, though, and I was only going to try it one time. My friend didn't want to do it to me because he knew my addiction would get worse after that. I convinced him I wanted to and it'd be okay. I could handle it. Finally, he did it for me. It was the most intense rush ever. It was the most amazing feeling and I can't even describe it. At that moment, I couldn't believe I had wasted so much time snorting it. I couldn't watch him put the needle in but I couldn't even feel It. Why had I not done this before? Okay so my friend was right... my addiction was about to get way worse.

Chapter 15

Addiction, Needles, and Lies

Oh my goodness. Where do I even begin? So much happened in this time period that some is a blur. I am going to try to put it in the best order I can but I have a feeling this is going to be all over the place. But then again, I was kind of all over the place. I want this to be as real as possible and share the real, hard facts of what it is like to be an addict. I will leave out some incriminating facts and use fake names. This is hard for me to put it all out there and it brings up a lot of memories, some good and some bad. It was a very bad time in my life and I did a lot of things I am ashamed of. I did everything that I said I would never do. I can't go back and change anything I did. Now I can look at it as a learning and growing experience and just make a better future for myself. It really has shaped me into the person I am today but I still have a past. I hope many people can see through what I did and see who I am now.

I am not sure what happened to my outpatient program at this point. I am thinking I quit going for a while, but I am not even sure. I was getting way deep into my addiction. I was working two full time jobs, King Burger and delivering pizzas. That was basically to be able to support my habits. I made cash every night delivering pizzas. Every single night when I got off work, I would go straight to the city to get heroin. I usually wouldn't go alone because I preferred not to put the needle in my own arm. I would have someone go and do this for me. I would always save just a little bit for the morning so I could make it through the day without getting sick. I couldn't function without heroin. I would be deathly ill. I would always take some to work with me and sometimes I would go shoot up in the bathroom at work. What if I would have overdosed in the bathroom at work or something? Who knows what could have happened? I made stupid choices. I never allowed myself to get sick. No matter what, I would find a way to get high.

Sometimes while I was working my day job, I would let people borrow my car to go down to the city and pick up for me. That way I would have some before I went to my other job. Then I would get off there and go down again. It was a never ending cycle. All I ever did was work, drive to the city and get high. I made that drive so many times every week, sometimes more than once a day. It was annoying driving down there all the time, but I didn't really care. I was going to do it and I was going to get high.

I remember going to the Cardinals game with my parents, sister, and brother in law and niece. It triggered me passing certain streets in the city on the way to the game. I couldn't stay there. I needed to get high. I could feel myself getting tense and angry. I barely made it to the start of the game and I called someone to come pick me up. The person who came to pick me up didn't get high. He knew I used to but he didn't know that I was. I had him drive all the way down to the city to pick me up. We went home and I hung out with him for a little bit. Then, I called my friend to go get high with me. I had to drive all the way back to the city but I needed it so bad. I couldn't wait any longer.

I remember one night I had to close at the pizzeria. It was a Saturday night and I didn't get off until one in the morning. That wasn't going to stop me from going to get heroin. My drug dealer was out of town and he had someone filling in for him. I had already talked to him and told the dealer when I would be off work. He was an older guy and he thought I was cute. He would make dirty comments towards me. He told me I needed to come alone or he wouldn't do it. This made me panic. I needed my drugs but I was scared to go alone. Why couldn't I bring anyone with me? What was he going to do to me? So my friends went down with me. I kept a knife in my pocket and I hid my friends in the trunk. Seriously, what was wrong with us? This is just one little piece of me putting myself in danger. I am lucky nothing bad ever happened to me.

I was constantly doing stupid things. I never thought about consequences. I only thought about how I would get high next. My life was a hot mess but I enjoyed the chaos. Anyone who didn't get high, I pushed out of my life, that or they pushed me out. I was able to hold myself together to work and look normal at work. I tried to hide it from everyone. My parents knew I was up to no good, but they didn't know I was doing heroin. I played things off pretty well. I would have to constantly be wearing long sleeves to hide my track marks. I would pick at my face and leave scars on my face. It looked horrible. I would wear a three quarter length shirt to work every day to hide my track marks. I would even have to wear long sleeves in the summer to cover them, no matter how hot it was. Sometimes I would have to shoot up in my hands and occasionally if my friends would miss, my hands would swell the size of a balloon. I had poor hygiene and I rarely showered since I was always on the go. I didn't take care of myself much at all.

It is so crazy to think about all the things I had to do and the lengths I had to go through to get high. I remember driving around delivering pizzas and shooting heroin in my arm while stopped at a stop sign. I said I would never share needles, but sometimes it was our only option. I overdosed numerous times. My friends would give me CPR and hope that I woke up. They would slap me and pour water on me to try bringing me back. Most of them wouldn't take me to the hospital because they didn't want to get into trouble. I had one friend who was always more worried about us living than getting into trouble. There were a couple of times I woke up on the way to the hospital. I am pretty sure I used up all nine of my lives.

My life was in a downhill spiral. It was getting bad. I don't even know what happened to my probation and my outpatient classes at this point. I believe I was on call in for my probation and I know I missed my outpatient classes. It eventually all caught up to me. I know I had dirty drops and I talked my way out of them. That only worked for so long. I used up my chances. One day I went into my class and we had to drop that day. I knew I was dirty and I knew it was my last chance. After I dropped dirty, my counselor talked with me. That was when they recommended I go to inpatient rehab. She wanted me to go right then but I talked her into letting me go the next day. I once again had to tell both of my jobs that I would be leaving for a little while. It was only for twenty one days and I was hoping they would understand. I also had to somehow find a way to tell my parents. They thought I was doing well, but I sure had them fooled.

Chapter 16

Inpatient Treatment

The night before I had to go to treatment, I stayed up all night getting high. I knew it didn't matter at that point, so I thought, why not? I packed my bags for the morning and I got up a little late. I finally got there shortly after I was supposed to be. I didn't tell my parents that I had to go to rehab. I drove myself there and I texted my mom before I walked in the door. I said, "I am going into rehab, I will be gone for three weeks. I will see you soon." Like I mentioned before, my parents thought I was doing well. They had no idea what or why. I turned my phone off, put it into the center counsel of my car and I went into rehab.

This was my second time doing an inpatient program. The first time was my prison stay and then I also had some of the outpatient program. I was absolutely pissed off. I went in there with a closed mind. I wasn't ready for this. When I first came in there, I was sick and I was tired. I had to go through a bit of an intake process. There I found out that I couldn't leave my car there. I would have to call my parents to come and pick it up. I wasn't ready to talk to them. I made the call and when my mom asked questions, I just ignored her. I told her I would explain later but they needed to come and get my car. I don't think they were happy.

After meeting with a counselor to go through intake process, the staff threw me right into some classes where I had to sit in uncomfortable chairs all day. I looked like hell. Everyone looked bad when they first came in off of the streets. I was quiet and I didn't talk to many people at first. I was scared and I was just not in the mood. I didn't want to go through the sickness. I wanted to go home. In my mind, I was planning my escape. I was trying to figure out a way that I could get myself out of there.

After a couple of days went by, my head began to clear some. I began to feel a little bit better as the dope sickness began to wear off. I was being more opened minded about being in the program. Maybe this was a good thing. I know I needed the help and that I couldn't do it on my own. This would give me enough time to try getting my act together and working a program. We barely were able to make phone calls at first and my parents were still probably wondering why I was even in rehab. They thought I was doing well and they were completely naïve to the situation.

I was talking to my counselor and I told her I felt it was time for me to tell my parents. We set it up so that I would tell them when they came to the visit. They would meet with me and my counselor so that she could be there for support and to help explain it to them. I was so nervous and as the day came closer I didn't know if I would be able to do it. What would they think? The day finally came and we had to wait until the afternoon to have our visits. The anxiety was killing me. I was so terrified.

The time finally came. My parents walked in and we sat to talk for a little bit. We went into my counselor's office and we all sat there together. It took a little time to work up the courage to tell them and I wouldn't look them in the eyes. I looked down at the floor as I blurted it out.

I believe it started something like this, "I know you guys are probably wondering why I am here. I have a problem with heroin." My voice was shaking as I spoke. I had done so many messed up things that my parents had kind of lost their shock value. In other words, nothing that came out of my mouth even surprised them anymore. I mean don't get me wrong, they were taken back by it. They also knew I had a lot of issues.

It was like a light bulb went off in their head and things were suddenly clear. They began to put things together like where all my money was going and why I looked the way I did. They began to ask questions and my counselor helped to fill them in. I know they were hurt. I know some tears were shed in that meeting. I know they felt like I was further and further away and they were losing their baby girl. I also know that they were happy I was in rehab. They were hoping that it would work this time. They just wanted me back.

After my parents left that day, I felt like a weight had been lifted off my shoulders. I more so told them so they could help me to stay clean. I wanted them to know certain warning signs and such so I wouldn't get high again. Later on, I was kind of mad at myself for filling them in. I was going to have to tell them something for why I was at rehab.

The rest of my time there I really tried to utilize all the information I learned. I thought this was it, that this would be the last time. I had it all figured out and I wanted to stay clean. One big thing the counselors tell you at rehab that you should always listen to is don't hang out with the same people and don't hang out with people you meet in rehab. It is not so much that you can't communicate with other addicts, but they don't want people who are freshly clean hanging out outside of rehab in the beginning. It is kind of like a domino effect. If one falls, they drag you down. I always hung out with people I met from prison and now from rehab. And I always ended up getting high with all of them.

I completed my twenty one days and I was ready to do this. This time felt different and I felt like I knew more. I wanted to do it for myself now and not anybody else. I had a few weeks of clean time to get me started and I just had to keep it going and continue down the same path.

This did not work for long.

Chapter 17

The Day I Died

Yes, you read that right. It does say the day I died. What does that even mean? How can you die but still be alive? Well, I guess that is the best way to put it because it was that close of a call. So close that I shouldn't even be here today or I should have permanent brain damage. This is the story of the day I died. I feel it is rather intense and graphic, but it shows the sick truth of what an addict goes through.

I had gotten out of rehab one week prior. This gave me a total of about four weeks clean time. I thought I was doing pretty well and I was on a roll. I was serious about doing it right this time. I wanted to stay clean. I know three weeks of my clean time was in a center, but I also had survived one week on my own. Even that was a big step for me. I was isolating myself from everyone, which is a good thing and a bad thing.

I was sitting at home watching television when a show about addicts came on. It is something that always interests me and, of course, the episode showed a girl who was addicted to heroin. This story looks rather familiar. I should have changed the channel right then and there, but instead I decided to torture myself. I watched as she shot up heroin and got high. Ugh, I started getting a sick and nauseous feeling. I wanted to get high. I got the urge and there was no going back. I was going to get high no matter what and nothing was going to change my mind. Rather than calling someone who could help me fight the craving and keep me from getting high, I called my buddy who I knew would get high with me.

I called up the dealer and I put my order in. I went and picked up my friend, down to the city we went. I was getting so anxious, I just couldn't wait to get high. I was getting so excited! We sat in our usual spot and waited for the dealer to arrive. Finally, after what felt like forever, he pulled up and the exchange was made. I wanted to get high right then, but my friend insisted that we should wait until we got home.

The drive felt like forever. I was extremely anxious and I couldn't wait any longer. We finally ended up pulling over into a parking lot in St. Charles. It was right off of Jung's Station Rd. I am not sure how we ended up there, but it was just a spot to pull into. I was going to get my fix. I got it all ready and I loaded up my syringe. Since I had been clean for a little while, I didn't do as much as I normally would. I was doing up to five or six pills at a time but this time I only did one and a half or two pills. I had my friend stick the needle in my arm. I watched as it filled with blood and he pushed it in. Ahhh, here comes the rush. I finally feel relief. It was time to go and get out of this parking lot.

Now this is the part I do not remember but this is pretty much how it went down. I began to drive to leave the parking lot and I blacked out at the wheel. I began to roll into an intersection at which point my friend threw my car into park. He tossed my deadweight body into the passenger's side and he basically stopped traffic to find out where the nearest hospital or anything was. He ended up following a lady to an ambulance base. He ran up to the door at the base and was banging on it. Then out came the paramedics. I am sure this was a rather random surprise for them. "Guy shows up at ambulance base with dead body in car." That sounds like a good headline to a news story. Obviously they didn't ask too many questions at first. They were more worried about saving my life.

They laid my dead body out on the cold ground. They went to work. They were trying to find a vein to pump me full of Narcan. Narcan is a drug used to reverse the effects of the opiates. They cut the sleeve to my hoodie and tried to stick it in my arm. As a heroin addict, I had ruined most of my veins. They could not find a place to put it in me and time was slipping away. I was moments away from being pronounced dead. I had just about reached the limit of going without oxygen. Finally, they were able to figure something out and they shot the Narcan into me. My body was not responding at first. I was closer and closer to death. They had to keep loading me up until finally I came to. I was extremely confused when I first opened my eyes. I was surrounded by people I didn't know. When I finally realized where I was and what had just happened, I was not even thinking about the fact I almost died. My immediate thoughts upon awaking were: oh shit I am going to be in trouble! OMG I can't believe they cut the sleeve on my brand new hoodie, and they totally just ruined my high! Thinking those thoughts just sounds sick to me. I also felt like I had been hit by a bus. My body was tense and sore. My head was pounding.

Now I do recall getting a slight lecture from the paramedics. "Do you realize what you just did to yourself? You were dead. You could have permanent brain damage. You are really lucky to be alive and not a vegetable. You need to evaluate your life." Maybe those weren't the exact words, but it was right along those lines. And to be honest, I kind of remember being ungrateful that they had saved me. I was not trying to commit suicide, but at this point in my life I had nothing to live for. I didn't care if I was dead or alive. It made no difference to me. I was still afraid I was going to be in trouble. I had already used up every last one of my chances and I knew the next time I screwed up the police would lock me up and throw away the key.

They put me in the back of the ambulance and covered me up. It was very cold outside and my body was in total shock. They checked my vitals and I believe they continued to lecture me. Next thing you know, here comes a sheriff knocking on the back door of the ambulance. Oh man, I wanted to break into tears. I thought this was it. As far as I knew, I was getting arrested again. I turned my head to the paramedics and said, "I'm in big trouble, aren't I?" The sheriff asked them if they needed assistance. They told him that they didn't need him. They had it under control. This was the first time I felt grateful in this whole mess. I thought to myself, "Hey, these guys aren't so bad after all."

Next, I am being taken to the hospital in the back of an ambulance. I did not want to go and I wanted to refuse, but they insisted. I had to stay for one hour for observation. I just wanted to go home. I wanted to get high. They ruined my high, talk about a buzz kill.

At the hospital I was wheeled in on the stretcher and put into a room. In come nurses and here comes more lectures. All of these grown-ups were telling me to evaluate my life. I have heard this a million times before. I just wanted to yell at them to leave me alone. It was my life and I could do whatever the hell I wanted to with it. It was none of anyone's business. Man, I was such a little bitch, I thought I was on top of the world and my shit didn't stink. As I laid in that hospital bed, I kept thinking about how I was going to tell my parents. I was on their insurance and I would have to pay for the ambulance ride as well as the emergency room visit. I figured I would nonchalantly throw it out there. I was the master of disappointment.

Finally, my hour was up and it was time to go home. Of course, I got one final lecture before leaving. It just went in one ear and out the other ear. My friend had my car and he came to pick me up. My first question was, where are the rest of my drugs? He had disposed of everything when the cops had come. I was looking forward to finishing that. That is so sick. I just overdosed and almost died, yet the only thing I could think about was getting high. The rest of the day I was sick from the Narcan. I was throwing up nonstop and was unable to keep down any food or liquids. My thoughts were, I can't believe they did this to me. I was always blaming everyone else, but I did it to myself.

The following day I had my outpatient treatment. I had a friend stay the night, someone in my class who I had met in inpatient. The situation was a hot mess. She was getting high and I guess some people react differently. I was up all night trying to keep her under control. She was doing all crazy stuff and basically sleep walking/hallucinating. I was trying to recover from my overdose and then I had to deal with that. I had zero sleep. It was morning time and it was time to go to class. I was trying to decide what I was going to do. I was hoping we wouldn't have to drop. Should I tell my teacher I overdosed? I have such a guilty conscience.

Here we are sitting in class. I probably look like hell. I died the day before, got no sleep and I was throwing up all day. We went around the room so everyone could share their piece. It landed on me. It was my turn to speak. I felt my stomach sink. I just blurted it out and put it out there, "I relapsed and I overdosed. I almost died and I was in the hospital. I am scared and I will never get high again."

My teacher's response, "First off, how long will that fear last for? It won't stay there forever. Second, what are we going to do? Nothing seems to be working and we need to find a solution. You have been in this outpatient program for a while now and you have continued to use. The next step after that was inpatient, which you just completed. Now, we are back at the beginning yet again."

"I know, I am really sorry, please just give me a chance. I know I can do this. I am scared. I don't want to get high again. It was a moment of weakness. I got it out of my system and I am ready to work my program." As addicts we are smooth talkers. We can make everything we say believable. We manipulate people until we get our way. I know that sounds horrible, but that is just the truth of it. And thank god she gave me another chance and didn't contact my probation officer. Well, that went over smoothly. I had one person down and now I just had to tell my parents. I guess I could use that same spiel.

I decided to tell my mom later that same day. That is a hard one. How do you tell a parent they almost lost their child? As angry as they were at me for all of my actions, they still loved me and they still wanted me safe.

I was getting ready to leave the house to go to work. "Hey, mom, I relapsed and I overdosed yesterday."

"What?!?"

"Yea, it is no big deal. I am scared now and I never want to get high again. I almost died and luckily I was saved by the paramedics. They had to take me to the hospital in the ambulance and we are going to have to pay for that. I am okay and there is nothing wrong with me. Well, I have to go to work now, bye." That is about how that went down. That is how much of a little shit I was. My mom was angry they weren't contacted but at the same time I wasn't a minor so they didn't need to be. I ran out the door and I went to work. As much as I wanted to get high, I knew I had to finish my outpatient program or I would be back in prison. I want to

92

say I stayed clean for a little bit or I just got high on the weekends. I was trying to give myself enough time between my classes for my system to clear out.

Now that you have read about how I felt about almost dying and how ungrateful I was, I will tell you my take on it today. I now look back at that situation and I just think I am crazy! This has been the hardest chapter for me to write in this book. It was extremely emotional for me. I can't believe that I almost died. This scene replays in my head rather often. I have to pass by the parking lot it happened in a lot and I still get sick when I pass by there. Today I think about how grateful I am that my friend wasn't worried about getting into trouble, he was more worried about my safety and making sure I was alive. I hate to say it but my friend who saved me is no longer with us today. He was one of my best friends and I miss him dearly. I wish I could have saved him, but I will get to that story later on.

I am beyond grateful for the paramedics saving me that day and not letting the cops arrest me. Looking back on their lectures and what they had to say to me, well, they were right. I was ruining my life and not even death could make me realize. I was in contact with one of the paramedics who did save me and I was planning to meet with him. I really wanted to as part of this story, but it hasn't worked out yet. As much as I want to, I am also terrified and I wouldn't even know what to say. I would just want to tell them how much I appreciate them and what they did for me that day.

Sometimes I wish I would have died that day, but I look at my life now and I thank God he wasn't ready for me yet. It was not my time to go and I am here to live and tell my story. I want to tell my story in hopes that I can save someone's life the way my life was saved.

Chapter 18

Fighting for My life

After I almost died, I did come to some realizations. I obviously had a problem and I did need help. I needed to make it through rehab classes and I needed to walk down (successfully complete) my probation. If I continued to do the same things, I wouldn't make it very far. There were only two options: prison or death. I tried to stay clean and do the right thing.

I did well for a little while. I continued my outpatient classes and I think I eventually got dropped down to once a week. I was in that program more than double the time it should take someone. I finally made it to once a week. The only problem with that was it gave me more freedom. Here we go again. The fight continues. At those classes, it was almost like a reunion with all my friends. I knew so many people who had to go through that program and I would run Into people I used to kick it with. That is when I started hanging out with Brad. He was just starting the classes or hadn't been in them for too long. I knew him from all the people I hung out with in high school, but to be honest I never liked him that much. I mean I did but he was good at making people mad.

One day this girl and I were leaving class. We were planning to go down to the city to get some heroin. Brad gave us some money to get him some also. We drove down there and waited for the dealer to meet us. We got our heroin and headed back to our side of town. We went to Brad's house and got high. At some point after that, Brad and I started dating. My friends weren't too happy when I told them. In fact, I tried to hide it for a little while. Again, this part in my life is a blur so I am going to try piecing it together the best I can.

I would stay at Brad's house a lot. We were both going to our classes at treatment and we were doing well keeping our addiction to the weekends. Neither of us could afford to get into trouble. We both had backgrounds. This worked for a while but, as we all know, heroin is not something you can do occasionally. Once again I was on a downhill spiral. Each time my addiction came back into full swing, it got worse.

The addiction began to get bad again. I was trying to be more sneaky and careful since now my parents knew the signs to look for. They found out quickly and I tried to have them help me get clean. I would give them my money so I couldn't spend it to go get high. I remember one night I was supposed to go deliver pizzas. I was so dope sick I was crying and my mom had to watch me miserable and in pain. She had some Vicodin for something and she let me have one to ease the pain so I could work. She wasn't doing it to hurt me. She was trying to help me and I begged for it. It was enough to ease the pain and get me through work. I ended up going and getting high after work. I couldn't handle the sickness.

I tried getting my life back in order, once again. I was trying something new. We contacted a doctor who prescribed Suboxone and a treatment in getting clean. My dad would take me to my appointments there. I would have to go pretty often and the doctor would make you take a drug test each time. They wouldn't give you the suboxone if you were still getting high. It helped to keep me from going through withdrawals and being sick. They wanted to control the substance and not let it be a street drug. A lot of people would sell it to make money to get high. I was actually doing well, again.

I decided to move out of my parent's house. I moved in with a friend and it was not too far from my house. When I first moved in there I was staying clean. I moved into my friend Brian's old room. This was a horrible idea. That room was the first place I stuck a needle in my arm and I spent many days high in that room. Just being in that room was a trigger. I am not sure why I thought I could stay clean living there. Also, being on my own, I had freedom. I didn't have to try to hide it from my parents anymore.

So I began getting high again, not shocking. I never was good at staying clean. The downward spiral began once again and it happened quickly. My boyfriend would stay with me most the time and we would get high together. I started not having rent money and he would have to help me to pay the rent. If there was a will, there was a way. I would find a way to get high no matter what. I was no longer able to get Suboxone. The doctor cut me off when I had dirty drug test. I only lived on my own for about four months I think, but a lot happened in a short amount of time. I was still working the same two jobs just to be able to pay my bills and support my habits.

I went to the hospital one day because I was feeling sick. After doing blood work, the nurses found out I had mono. It was a great excuse to get high, miss work, and not go to my outpatient rehab. It gave me a doctor's note and I rode it out. My boyfriend was mad at first, wondering how I got mono. I guess because they call it the kissing disease. I am guessing I had just run my immune system down.

I was supposed to be at work one day but I didn't have any dope at all. I was so ill, I was throwing up and using the restroom a lot. I was sweating and I had the chills. I was curled up in the fetal position just crying. I was kicking and screaming. I didn't want to move, but I couldn't stay still. I felt like I was dying! My boyfriend wasn't there and I called him to help me. We were trying to get clean at that time but as usual it wasn't working out. He told me to just say the word and he would help me. So I did and he couldn't get back soon enough. I was so sick. He came in and I remember I couldn't find a spot to put it because my veins weren't cooperating. I remember lying face down on the bed and having to do it in the back of my leg. It was instant relief. I was suddenly all better. It is crazy to think of how sick you can get from lack of drugs. It is not just a mental addiction; it is physical. Your body has to have it.

While we were living in this house, Brad and I were so back and forth with our relationship. Our relationship was based off drugs and it was the cause of all of our fights. One week one of us would be trying to get clean and the other would be getting high. It was different from week to week in who played which role. One week, I was the one who wanted to get clean. I took all of our syringes and I went and threw them in a gas station trash can. My boyfriend flipped when there were no needles to get high. I bitched about it because I didn't want to get high. Of course, I finally gave in. Then I was freaking out on how we would get our syringes. It was up to me to fix it. I went to where I threw them away but the trash had been emptied. There was another time I had to dig my syringe out of a trash can at Green's because I changed my mind. Luckily, I was able to purchase them at Green's. Sometimes it would work and sometimes it wouldn't. It was always easier to get them in the city. We got high and our fight ended. We fought a lot and like I said it was all based off drugs. I would get mad at how he would act high and he didn't like how I acted high. We were poison for each other but we thought we were in love.

We were seriously messed up in the heads. I think most people would agree to this. One day we had the brilliant idea that we should have a baby. I thought it sounded like an awful idea at the time. We put together a master plan, though. We were going to have a baby, get clean and get married. It sounded like a good idea in our minds at the time. I can laugh about this now but really what were we thinking? It didn't work well for us. Anyone with a clear head would get clean, get married and then talk about babies. We did it in the wrong order and we didn't even end up staying together. That will come later.

While getting high again, I managed to violate my probation. I don't even remember exactly what it was. I just know I got a letter listing out everything I did wrong from dirty drops to not following my stipulations. It had finally caught up to me. This letter I got did not look good on my part at all. I just remember I ended up in jail and handcuffed to that bench at St. Charles county jail once again. I was sitting there and staring at the same corrections officers who would take their time. I had a higher bail and I was trying to convince my parents or my boyfriend to get me the hell out of there. There was no way that was happening.

I was going through the booking process and I was going through the medical portion. The nurse asked all of the usual questions and she asked when my last menstrual cycle was. It had been more than a month, but with my drug use it was always irregular. She wanted to do a pregnancy test just in case. I was just like whatever, I know I am not pregnant but I will take it anyway. I peed in the cup and gave it to her. They put me back on the bench. A few minutes later she came back in to tell me my test was positive. I was just thinking you have got to be kidding me. This isn't a funny joke. Because of my drug use, I had to be transported to the hospital to be checked out. A correctional officer took me to the hospital in my oranges with ankle cuffs and handcuffs. It was the worst.

I called my mom from the jail phone. That was when I told her I had found out I was pregnant. It was probably not the best way to find out that your daughter Is expecting a child. It wasn't really the best circumstances. I don't think my parents were too thrilled about the news. Again, not much I did really shocked them anymore. They didn't like my boyfriend either so that just made it worse.

I spent a good amount of the day in booking and going to the hospital. I can't remember if I ended up going down to a pod or not. I want to say I did for a day or two but then I was released with a court date. My court date was set about five months from that day I got out.

Chapter 19

Pregnant

So here I am, out and about, and pregnant. This was not a good idea. I was hoping being pregnant could change me, but it didn't work. Eventually it did, but not at first. I continued to smoke cigarettes. I just couldn't quit. I always looked down on people who smoked while they were pregnant. I always thought it was stupid not to quit, but now I understood. It is not that easy. I also hate to say it, but the same went for drugs. I couldn't quit. I continued to use heroin. I did cut down to smaller doses and my reasoning was that I did not want to miscarry. A lot of times when people would quit using heroin when they found out they were pregnant, they would miscarry. The baby would go through withdrawals. I didn't want that to happen. In all reality, I just couldn't give up drugs.

To this day, I feel so guilty about this. It hurts me to know that I did this. I am so lucky I have a happy, healthy child. Anytime something does go wrong with him or his behavior, I feel it is my fault and that I messed him up. He is so smart, though, and he is a healthy growing toddler. I also feel guilty knowing that so many people don't do anything during their pregnancy but their kids have medical issues. I think I will always beat myself up for this no matter what. It is hard for me to even admit this. It just goes to show how much control the addiction had over me. As I mentioned before, I did all the things I said I would never do. All the things I looked down on others for, I ended up doing.

I spent this time working and trying to do the right thing. I never really had morning sickness through my pregnancy. I just remember being lethargically tired. I just wanted to sleep. I was still working both jobs and I was still using drugs. I was going to my outpatient classes and I had moved back home with my parents. I was still with Brad and we thought we were ready for what was to come. We had a lot of ups and downs through this time. We were trying to plan our lives as parents, but we had no clue where to even begin. We were absolutely clueless and we couldn't even stop getting high.

Five months later, it was time to appear in court. It was August 12, 2010. I wasn't really showing much at this time. My belly just barely stuck out. I was ready and I wasn't expecting anything bad to come out of it. I thought my lawyer had it worked out. I also thought since I was pregnant that I would get away with it. I should have known better. Every time I appeared in that court room, I never went home. I always left in handcuffs with a sheriff. I didn't plan for it at all. I was sentenced to one hundred and twenty days in St. Charles County Jail. That was way worse than going to prison. I didn't want to spend all of that time in county. I was absolutely pissed! Their reasoning for locking me up that day was for the protection of the unborn child. It would keep me from getting high and doing bad things during my pregnancy. Yes, I understand that but I was not happy. Looking back now, it was the best thing that could have happened to me. Otherwise I know I would've continued to get high through the rest of my pregnancy.

It was an emotional moment as I was put in those handcuffs. I cried my eyes out and both my parents got to see me leaving that court room in handcuffs, again. My mom was crying as well. There was a reason I was put in jail that day. I was upset because I was supposed to find out the sex of my baby in a few days. Now I would have to wait. As mad as I was at that time, I am so thankful that I spent my pregnancy in jail. I was planning to leave that court room and go get high. I do not have the best memory of being pregnant but it was by far the safest place for me.

I was handcuffed and transported over to the jail. I was upset and I didn't want to be there. I couldn't stop crying. I would spend my whole pregnancy there and get released two weeks before my due date. I had to go through the booking process and change out into my county oranges. When going through medical the nurses at the jail had asked me about my drug use. They said it was important to be honest for the safety of my baby. Yes, I was using, but I was not using very much so I didn't think I would even withdrawal or get sick. I told them I hadn't been using. I really didn't want to go to the hospital again and I really didn't want to take methadone during my pregnancy.

I was taken down to my pod and placed in my cell. The one good thing about being pregnant was that I got the bottom bunk. I also got an extra mattress for my bed. It still was not the most comfortable. Over the next couple of days, I did get a little bit sick. It was a small withdrawal and nothing to be alarmed over. It went really fast. I think it was also a combination of stress from being put in jail. Since I was pregnant, I also got an extra snack at night. It was usually a cheese sandwich, some fruit and two cartons of milk. Sometimes the officers would forget about it and I would have to go ask for it. I would only drink water from the ice buckets. The faucet water tasted like lead. If they didn't bring it I wouldn't drink water at all. I would feel sick and tired from dehydration.

It took me a little while to grasp the concept that I was going to be here for the next four months. I was not mentally prepared for it but I knew I had to prepare myself otherwise I would be miserable. There was nothing I could do to change the situation I was in. It could have been worse. I was lucky I was getting out before I had my son. I could have gone to prison and had to serve my back up of eight years. I am lucky with what I got although I didn't see it at the time.

The very first letter I received from my mom was painful. It was the truth and it was harsh. She didn't mean it in a bad way, but it really hurt me. After everything I did to hurt my parents, I understand why she felt the way she did. When I read it now, it still hurts. I still feel guilty today about everything I did to my parents and how badly I hurt them. So here is that first letter she wrote me:

Dear Jamie,

I hope you are doing ok and you are eating good and getting the care you need for the baby. I am very upset over what has happened, but honestly I am not sure it isn't for the best. I truly am not convinced that you were staying clean, even being pregnant. I am so scared about the health and well-being of the baby. When Brad came over and we talked about it, he didn't even try to convince us, his comment was, "Well she wasn't with me all the time." He lied to us about the money. I think it will give you some time to reflect on your life and if you are responsible and ready to raise a child. I honestly don't think your boyfriend is. He has a lot of issues to deal with and a lot of growing up to do. I am sorry if I am being harsh but I went from nonstop crying to being angry that we are dealing with a child's life being at risk. I love you so much and I want you to change and get your life in order. I want you to think long and hard about what kind of mom you will be. If you can't give this baby what it deserves, then as much as it pains me to say this, maybe you should think about adoption, or even your dad and I adopting. If you truly feel you can be the best mom you can be to the baby, then your dad and I are behind you 100% and will do what we can to help you. I will try to find every means of help I can. Dad and I have talked about finances. When you start working, we are going to have to take control of your money. We can figure out an allowance, but you are going to have to save money. How are you even going to buy diapers? It makes me so angry that your boyfriend owes you money and he said your friend owes you money too. You can't even pay your own bills; I don't understand why you would even loan money to anyone. Brad gave us twenty dollars but I think we will just take care of it from here. I am having a really hard time dealing with this and I am sorry but I feel like you and he have both continually lied to us. I will get thru this but right now I am angry with everyone ---- including God. I feel like I have been let down. I am hoping you come out of there a stronger and better person because you are truly a beautiful girl with so much to give. I know if you can beat all of this you will be an awesome mom. I hope there are some parenting books in there for you to read. I hope your pregnancy is an easy one and I pray to God your baby is healthy. Hang in there and we will see you next week. I really miss you and I wish I could just pick up the phone and call you. Take care and know that I am thinking about you all the time and I love you so much.

Love you,

Mom

P.S. On a positive note, at least you won't have to spend any money on maternity clothes.

Well, that was not an easy read. It hit home and brought tears to my eyes. The thought of adoption and being an unfit mother was the harsh reality of it. I couldn't even take care of myself, let alone another human being. She was right. Was I ready to be a mom? I didn't know what I was dealing with. I had a long time to reflect though and grow as a person. Jail was the best place for me at that time. I spent those four months bettering myself as a person. I formed a new outlook on life while I was in there.

After being there for a little while I was able to go to the doctor's office and find out the sex of my baby. I wanted a boy so badly. I would have been happy either way, but I was really hoping for a boy. My doctor's visits were rather interesting. I had to go sit in booking until the officers were ready to take me. They would put me in handcuffs and ankle cuffs. I was also wearing my county oranges. I would then be transported to the doctor's office. It was a normal office outside of the jail. All of the people would stare at me like I was some sort of monster. People make mistakes. It doesn't make you a bad person. How would you feel if you were sitting at the doctor's office and you see an inmate escorted in by an officer? I think it is in our nature to stare, judge and be scared.

After what seemed like the longest wait ever, I was taken back for my ultrasound. I was so nervous and excited. That is when the doctors told me I was having a boy. I cried tears of joy and I couldn't wait to tell Brad and my parents. After I was able to tell everyone, they were all excited, too. My sister had a daughter and was also pregnant with another girl. My baby would be the first boy. We had originally picked out a few names but we couldn't agree. We agreed on Kash but he wanted to spell it with a "C" and I wanted to spell it with a "K". At that point, I had thought of giving my son his dad's last name, but so much changed in those four months. Four months doesn't seem like a long time, but when you are sitting there all day long staring at the same walls with nothing to do, it seems like a life time.

It was not easy to be pregnant in jail. I feel like I missed out a lot on the happiness of pregnancy. I know it was the best place for me to be and it truly was the safest place for the baby. You don't think about the little things though. I only got one ultrasound of my baby while I was in jail. If I had a food craving, well I did not get to fulfill it. I didn't get to choose what I was able to eat. I have no pictures of my belly as I went through different trimesters. My doctor's appointments were not with my doctor and I was always chaperoned by a correctional officer. I didn't get to sleep comfortably in my own bed. It is hard to look back at my pregnancy and have these things as my memories. I think one day down the road if the circumstances are right that I want to have another baby. I want to be able to enjoy my pregnancy and all of the little things that come with it.

The visits started out with both Brad and my parents coming. They would take turns coming in. Every time my boyfriend came he was high. It began to really irritate me. I don't know if I was more mad that I couldn't get high or the fact that he needed to change for our son. Maybe I never would have changed or felt that way if I hadn't been locked up. As I was in jail, I knew I needed to change my life. It was the first time I actually felt ready. After a couple visits of him being high, I got angry and took him off of the visitor's list. I was also getting mad because I was hardly getting any mail from him. I was in jail and pregnant with his child. He could have made more of an effort. It was our decision to have a baby so we could change our lives. I broke up with him and cut him out of my life.

In the time I cut him out of my life, I did a lot of life reflecting. I was trying to figure out a career path and figure out what I was going to do when I got out of jail. I knew I was going to be a single mom, but I also knew that I had my parents by my side. I changed the name back to what I originally wanted it to be but he didn't like it. I decided on naming our son "Kingston" and I also decided he would have my last name. Everyone always asks me where I got the name Kingston from. In reality it is because I love reggae music and that is why I liked to so much. I also feel it is a strong name and it is different. I talked to a lot of people in there who had been through similar issues with their kid's dads. I learned a lot on the best things to do and I had a lot to think about.

After a couple of months of feeling lonely and weak, I sent Brad a letter. It was a moment of weakness where I felt emotional. I was listening to my radio and a song by Colbie Cailait came on called, "I Never Told You." The song reminded me of him and our situation. There was a lyric in the song that said, "I see your blue eyes, every time I close mine." He had blue eyes and it just brought tears to my eyes and made me think of him. Maybe it was dumb but I knew we would have to make something work somehow. I had him come visit me for a little bit and we talked some more. I don't think many people were happy about this. It was confusing for me and I wanted to make things work for our baby.

While I was in jail, I made some good friends who really helped me through a lot. It was a hard time in my life and I was lucky to have crossed paths with them. Today I still talk to one person who I met. Her name is Amber and I will always consider her a wonderful friend even though we don't always talk. She helped me so much and I am thankful that she came into my life. She really taught me a lot and I was glad we were able to room together. I am happy to say that she is still clean and doing awesome. She is an amazing mother to two beautiful kids.

Finally, after four long months it was time to go. The day couldn't come soon enough. I was so afraid my baby was going to come early. I didn't want to have him and then have to go back to jail until I was released. I was huge and pregnant. My parents came to pick me up and they brought me some baggy sweatpants and a t shirt. I knew the same clothes I wore into jail were not going to fit me. I was so excited to see the outside world other than my doctor's appointments. From the jail we had lots to get done. We had to go to the Medicaid office to get insurance for my son. I set up an appointment to go see my actual doctor who would be delivering my baby. We were planning my baby shower which my mom had to do a lot of while I was gone. It is hard when you are locked up and trying to take care of these things. My parents had to do a lot of planning and prepping. I am so thankful for everything they did. They even had a room painted and decorated for him.

That evening when I got out of jail, I went over to Brad's house. We obviously had a lot to talk about and I wasn't even sure where we stood at that time. We had a love/hate relationship. I was angry with him, but I was also excited to see him. I was also excited to see his parents and for them to see my belly, too. I knew we were all looking forward to the baby coming.

Chapter 20

Birth of My Son

It was getting close and I was ready to pop. I was so uncomfortable and I couldn't wait to give birth. My due date was December 28, 2010. I wanted to have my son before the new year. My sister was in town and I wanted to have him while she was there so she and her husband could meet the baby. I went to the doctor and we decided to get me induced. Otherwise, Kingston probably wouldn't have made his appearance until after the first of the year. I went into the hospital on the 27th and the doctors began labor inducing. After a while they gave me Pitocin. Labor progressed rather slowly that day. It wasn't until the next day that things began moving.

My family was up visiting me and hanging out with me. I was having rather painful contractions but it wasn't as bad as I imagined it would be. I had messaged my boyfriend the day before letting him know I was being induced. He didn't show up until later in the afternoon on the 28th. It was absolutely the most embarrassing thing when he finally did show up. He was so high, I couldn't even have a normal conversation with him. It was so bad that when he went to smoke a cigarette the nurse came in the room to talk to me about him. The medical staff didn't feel it was safe for him to be around in that state of mind. They had a security guard stop him from coming back into the hospital. My parents, of course, were not happy about it, but we just moved on. We didn't want to stress me out anymore.

Labor was moving along but not super quick. We were making progress, though. Of course, after the incident with Brad, I did receive a couple of text messages. I blew them off. He did that to himself and I would not feel sorry for him. My mom and best friend Brittany were the ones in the room with me. I was thankful for that. I was given an epidural and the doctors broke my water. It was the weirdest feeling ever. I was embarrassed because I thought I just kept on peeing. It was so gross. Finally, after what seemed like forever, they told me to push. I was scared but excited. I pushed for so long that the epidural was wearing off and the anesthesiologist had to come and give me another shot. It was a total of three hours that I pushed. He just did not want to come out. The doctor ended up pulling him out with the forceps.

That is when it happened. I heard that first cry and the doctor set him on me for the first time. I broke out into tears of joy. It was the happiest and most emotional moment of my life. I can't even describe what I felt. Kingston James Stewart was born on December 29, 2010 at 1:50 a.m. He was 8 lbs. and 5 oz.; yeah, he was always a big boy. He was absolutely perfect. He had a head full of blonde hair and beautiful blue eyes. He had a black eye from the forceps. I couldn't believe I had made something so perfect. My life changed forever at that moment.

The next day I messaged Brad's parents and let them know the baby was born and they could come visit whenever. They did not know their son wasn't present for the birth and hadn't met him yet. I had quite a few visitors that day. My parents were there as much as they could be but they both had to work. Brittany came back later that day when she got off work. My sister, her husband and my niece also came to visit. It was later in the afternoon when Brad's parents came. It was his parents, his sister and her girlfriend. They didn't know what had happened yet. They asked where he was and I just got silent. I told them that he had shown up but he was high and had gotten kicked out of the hospital. They were furious and called him. Of course, he made up a story. They asked me about having him come up to see the baby. I was angry but I agreed as long as one of his parents came with him. Later that evening, Brad and his dad came up. It was a little awkward at first but things were fine after that. Luckily, he was gone when the birth certificate was filled out. I gave my son my last name and I left him off. I knew it was the best choice that day and I am glad with the decision I made.

It was finally time to leave the hospital. I gathered up all of my belongings and I got Kingston dressed and ready. It was cold outside so I bundled him up. They wheeled me out of the hospital with Kingston in his car seat on my lap. My dad was the one to take me home. I was so excited to go home and sleep, or should I say lie in my own bed. I knew it meant I wouldn't be getting much sleep and I had a lot in store for me. I guess I was as ready as I was ever going to be.

Chapter 21

I am a New Mom

Wow, being a new mom is a lot of work and stressful. I was sore from giving birth and my legs were so swollen it hurt to walk. I didn't swell during my pregnancy, just after. I was absolutely exhausted. Taking a shower or a nap seemed like a luxury. I wasn't working at the time. I was just adjusting to being a new mother. My parents were there to help me. I remember waking up in the night and just wanting to cry when I couldn't get Kingston back to sleep. I remember going into my parents' room saying, "I need help!" I felt bad because they were actually working and I wasn't doing anything other than taking care of Kingston. They were always willing to help me, though.

I was beginning to feel rather depressed. I don't think I had a major case of postpartum or anything, but I was having a hard time adjusting. It was stressful and overwhelming. I spent my pregnancy in jail, got out and two weeks later I had a baby. It was a lot to take in and it didn't help that me and Kingston's dad had problems. I always tried to give him a chance, though. At that time, I went against my parents and friends; I still tried. I continued to see him even after the hospital incident. He was the father of my child and I always pictured myself having a perfect little family. I liked his parents and I wanted them to be able to be a part of his life as well. The whole situation in general was difficult. It was a lot for me to process. Sometimes Kingston and I would stay the night over there. My parents were never happy about this and I don't blame them. They were protective over us. Brad and I never gave them much of a reason to trust us. I didn't have the best track record and they were afraid I was going to fall back into my old habits. I will admit that I did start smoking cigarettes again. I was stressed and I think about a month into it, I caved.

After my five to six weeks were up and I was cleared to work again, I went back to working at King Burger. I was able to work my schedule around my parent's schedules so my dad would watch him in the evenings. Sometimes Brad's parents would also watch him. It was a pay check and I was so glad I had my parents help. I finally decided it was time to figure out something to do with my life. Believe it or not, I was always into nutrition and I always had a goal of being a dietician. I looked around at schools and I tried to figure out my options. All the programs for being a dietician seemed rather expensive and like a lot of school. That is when I came across a fitness trainer program at Missouri College. I investigated that more and it seemed like a perfect fit for me, or at least close enough to what I wanted to do. The times of the classes worked perfectly and I started my enrollment process. I filled out an application and I met with an advisor.

I had started to work on my own health and something that would make me happy. I needed an outlet. I wasn't doing much other than working and being a mom. I was isolated. I decided to start running. I always wanted to do a 5K and I wanted to find some people who would do it with me. I convinced my sister and her husband to run my first 5K with me. It was the Chesterfield Turkey Trot on Thanksgiving day in 2011. It was about a week before that race that I ran 3 miles, just to make sure I could do it. I was still new at running and I decided to jump in head first. I had been working out at a gym and taking classes, but I hadn't run much. I was also still smoking cigarettes at that time. It was finally the day of the race and I was so excited that I ran the whole thing without stopping. My sister's husband is a Marine so he finished it the fastest out of the three of us and my sister was in the same boat as me. I was excited that I finished in 32:30. I was super proud of myself and felt awesome. I fell in love with running from that day forward. I can't explain exactly what it was that I felt that day. I felt like it was a huge accomplishment for me and I was so proud of myself. The whole race experience was amazing to me and the endorphin high from running became addictive. At least this time I was becoming addicted to something healthy. After this day I knew that I wanted to keep doing this. There was no stopping me now.

Chapter 22

The Beginning of Something New

I started school in November of 2011. I was almost unable to go because of my felonies. It was hard enrolling and I had to go in knowing that I couldn't take the certification test offered through my school because I was a felon. I was glad the school let me take my chances, though. I knew there were other certifications that I could get. I knew getting a job was not a guarantee for me, but because my mom owns a fitness studio, I knew I had other options. I still wanted to get an education and I was hopeful that things would work out. That is just one of the obstacles I have to deal with in my life today, the fact that my past is permanently on my record. It is so aggravating dealing with that. I have changed so much, but it is hard for people to look past that. I am immediately judged off that and it is like people don't want you to better yourself. I won't let it hold me back, though. I was excited that I was still able to go to school.

I went to school every Monday and Wednesday from eight in the morning until five in the evening. It was about a thirty minute drive, but luckily it was only two days a week. It was a bummer that I hit rush hour traffic both ways. I was excited to be doing something new with my life and I was ready to learn. I was feeling more motivated than ever. It was a lot to handle with having a baby at home, but I always had help to get through it. Kingston began to go to daycare on the days I had school. I was so nervous with him being in daycare but I knew it was good for him and it was only two days a week.

I continued to run more and work on my health. After all, I was going to be a fitness trainer so I had to be healthy myself. After running for a while, I finally decided it was time to quit smoking. It is funny that every time after I went for a run the first thing I would do when I finished was smoke. That doesn't make sense to me but at the time I loved it. I knew it was time to quit, though. It wasn't easy at first, but once I decided I was ready then it was easy. I just had to do it cold turkey. I know that I am an all or nothing kind of person. I just quit. The hardest part was adjusting to certain habits of when and where I would always smoke. I just had to stay busy and keep my mind busy. I was constantly running around to stay busy. I was amazed at how quickly my lungs recovered and how much I could tell in my running.

I was feeling happier than ever. Life was going great. I had never felt this kind of happiness In my life ever before. It was confusing that I was actually happy. I spent so many years being sad and depressed. As far as Kingston's dad goes, that was very back and forth. We would get along and hangout sometimes or we wouldn't talk at all. I didn't trust him to watch Kingston alone, so if I did I would make his parents be there. I really tried to let him be a part of Kingston's life even though everyone else thought I was stupid for trying. That is when a couple of events ruined it for me. One day I was over there and I found a syringe on the floor in his room. His parents and Kingston were out in the other room. I was so angry. I went and grabbed Kingston and said, "We are leaving." His mom asked what was wrong and I told her what I found. They were also angry. Brad tried convincing me that he wasn't getting high and it was old. Either way, I couldn't have my son around that. I couldn't have my son in an unsafe environment.

His parents were even drug testing him at that point. There were other times I thought he was getting high but he convinced me he wasn't. I wasn't stupid, but he tried to make me feel like the bad guy for making accusations. His parents drug tested him that day and it came back clean. I thought there was absolutely no way. I found out later that he had rigged the tests they had. One day I even went and bought a drug test but he left before I got back.

I let him watch Kingston a few times under the supervision of an adult. Then I found out he had been getting high the whole time. I was so angry. At that point I pulled Kingston from his life and I cut him out completely. I felt like such an idiot. I felt like everyone was looking at me and saying, "I told you so." I tried to be nice and I tried to give him a chance. I had to do what was best for my son. I didn't want to risk anything happening to him. We moved on with our lives and I was thankful I had my parents by my side.

I continued to go to school and I was really enjoying it. I also began to become a workout fanatic and a health nut. In fact, I would probably say it became an addiction and for a while I overdid it. I was running a 5K nearly every weekend. I also added in some 10K's as well. I dropped seven minutes off of my 5K time within six months. I got a bit too skinny as I became obsessed. I absolutely loved racing and the way that it made me feel. I was so excited when I took third place overall female at a race and got a plaque for it. I decided I wanted to sign up for a half marathon next because I wanted a new challenge. I had no idea what I was getting myself into.

Everything was going great at this point. I was so happy, positive and full of life. I had never felt better. I was enjoying everything that was going on in my life. I loved going to school and learning and I loved my new healthy lifestyle. I loved being a mom more than anything. Life was perfect. I felt like a completely new person. I had been away from drugs for quite some time now. I believe it was close to two years at this point. I can't say it was always easy, but I was way more responsible and I was able to think about the consequences if I ever gave in to a trigger.

I was running a lot more and I was training for my first half marathon. A friend of mine had told me about an organization called Team in Training. It is an endurance sports program where you raise money for The Leukemia and Lymphoma Society while being coached to do an endurance event. I thought it sounded like an awesome idea so I looked into it. I signed up to do the Walt Disney World Marathon. I figured if I was going all the way to Disney I was going to do the full, all or nothing. We had group trainings and I had a coach named Doug. I followed his training plan which was great since I was still fairly new to running. This was completely different than running a 5K. I needed all the extra help I could get. We also did lots of fundraising and I had a certain minimum to fundraise. I had to raise $3,500.00. I enjoyed doing this a lot because it was something that made me feel good about myself helping such an amazing organization. It was hard fundraising, training, working and being a mom. I enjoyed staying busy and I met a lot of really cool people along the way. We would fundraise downtown at sporting events and also outside of grocery stores. You meet some very generous people and hear a lot of stories how people could relate. You would hear some good cancer stories and some bad cancer stories. I enjoyed hearing the good stories and the bad ones always gave me the chills. It was heart-breaking but reminded me of why I was doing what I was doing.

I hadn't run my half marathon yet, but it had fallen into my training for my full. It was on October 5, 2012, in St. Charles. It was the Cowbell Half Marathon, a nice flat and fast course. It was perfect weather, started out a little cold but warmed up. I was nervous but I knew I had put the training in so I was ready. My parents and Kingston came to cheer me on. They were around mile

118

5 and I sure was excited to see them there. I was feeling good and I kept on running. I finished the race in 2:05:40. I felt good about my time for my first half marathon. It was such a huge accomplishment for me and it meant so much more than running a race. It was about everything I had overcome and putting that medal on was a brand new beginning for me. I was excited to continue this lifestyle. I loved the runner's high more than the high from any other drug.

Chapter 23

July 2012

I know I am slightly back tracking, but I feel this memory needed its own chapter. It was something that was extremely hard for me to deal with and I still struggle with it today.

It was mid-July and I was at work one day. I had given my manager the headset so I could use the bathroom. Of course, I checked my phone while I was in there. I always did. I was scrolling through Facebook. A friend of mine posted something like: "For those of you who don't know, RIP Brain." I immediately freaked out. I looked at the comments. My response was WTF? I burst into tears. I tried to get it together to go back to work but I couldn't stop crying. I walked out of the bathroom crying and I tried to take the headset back. My manager asked what was wrong.

Through my tears I blurted out, "My best friend died." I was crying uncontrollably and she told me to take a second to get myself together. I tried to get it together and I was able to block out as much of it as I could until I got off work. I was having a hard time dealing with it. I hadn't talked to him much in a while because I was clean and he was still getting high. We would still talk, though. He was always the one person I could talk to that I went to for everything. Still today anytime anything good or bad happens, he is the first person I want to talk to. I would just love to hear his voice one more time.

One of the hardest parts of this for me is the fact that he saved my life. He was the one who took me to the paramedics when I was almost pronounced dead. I wish I could have been there for him. I will never forget about him and I think about him rather often. He was taken way too young. I will always miss him.

Chapter 24

2013- The Year of Marathons

After all of that running and training, the day had finally come to run my first full marathon. I traveled down to Florida with my team. It was in January, so it was nice to go somewhere warm. I was so nervous but I was so excited. I can't even describe the emotions I was feeling. I made sure I was well rested, but that is hard to do the night before a race. We had to be at the starting line at like three in the morning or something crazy. Then we had to wait forever.

The race had so many corrals, so the people further back had to walk forever just to get to the starting line. They also had a much longer wait. I was in the second or third corral. It was finally our time to start. I just started easy and tried to keep a nice pace. I ran with my friend Amanda until about mile sixteen. She stayed with me and she helped me so much. She encouraged me to keep going. She helped to make the first part seem easy. The more miles I added on, the harder it became. I tried to keep it to where I only walked at water stations but towards the last six miles or so I had to walk a little bit more.

This was definitely the best experience for a first marathon. We got to run through all four Disney parks. I was taking pictures as I ran and it was amazing. I can't even describe it. As I got closer to the end, there were crowds of people cheering. When I crossed the finish line I almost broke into tears of joy. I couldn't believe what I had just done. I was also a bit angry and snappy. I was mad because people stopped right in front of me and I needed to keep my legs moving. The race directors put that medal around my neck and I once again felt so proud of myself and what I had accomplished. I went from a heroin addict to a marathon runner and I had never felt happier. I felt as if I had overcome so much to get to that point. I was on a runner's high for a week. I couldn't wait to do more. I finished my first marathon in four hours and forty five minutes.

My next race was a half marathon in April in St. Louis. I ran that one in about the same time as my first half marathon. I was a full on running addict. I then wanted to try something new and I knew some people who did triathlons. I joined the St. Louis Triathlon Club. I grew up swimming all year round so that was easy for me and I was already running. Now, I just had to learn about riding a road bike. I figured riding a bike would be a piece of cake. I bought a road bike off of someone. I will never forget the first time I rode it. I was terrified! I held onto the brakes the whole time I went down a hill. I felt very unsteady and I was scared of cars. I think I only rode about six or seven miles that day. It felt like so much more. I thought I had good endurance from running, but riding a bike was completely different. In order to get better at biking and stay involved with Team in Training, I joined the Tucson Century team. I started riding a lot more and I was getting a lot more comfortable.

In the Spring of 2013, I got hired on at Silver's Gym as a personal trainer. I had finished school in November of 2012. I thought I had landed my dream job. I stayed at King Burger until I was able to build clientele at the gym. I was absolutely terrified being a trainer. It was something new and the gym was intimidating to me. It took me a little bit of time to get more comfortable. I loved working there, though, because I could always workout. I was always there and I had no excuse. There was also a pool so I was able to swim a lot more.

I signed up to do my first triathlon at New Town in July of 2013. I forget the exact distance of the swim but it was just a little short of an Olympic distance, then a 24 mile bike ride followed by a four mile run. The anxiety before the race was killing me. I had been training but at the same time this was much different than just running. I was still scared of the bike and I was terrified of anything going wrong on the bike mechanically. I felt like I did awesome for my first triathlon, though. My time was 2:06:15 and I felt so awesome when I finished. Again, it was a huge accomplishment for me and it was something new. I began to love the idea of multisport and I wanted to do more.

I did so many races in the year 2013. I ran the Cowbell Marathon in October and I hit a PR (personal record) of 4:28 and some seconds. I didn't walk once and again I felt amazing. Every medal I collected meant something to me. I can't describe how emotional every race finish is for me knowing how far I have come. I did the Rock n' Roll Half Marathon at the end of October. I ended up with drawling from the Tucson cycling team and I switched over to run another full marathon. I just didn't have the time for the training and fundraising. I was also dealing with some stomach issues and I didn't think I was going to be able to race at all. Luckily, it got somewhat better for a while. I ran the Bass Pro Marathon in Springfield, Missouri, in November. That was just a month after my last marathon. That was when I learned about a group called Marathon Maniacs. You had to run a certain amount of marathons in a certain amount of days to qualify. My friend and I decided we had to join and we had already run two. We just needed to find one more to run. We found a marathon called Run for the Ranch back in Springfield, Missouri, in December. She was already near there staying with family. I woke up early and my mom drove me down there to run the marathon. My friend and I stayed together the whole time and it hurt. We crossed that finish line holding hands and were so proud of our accomplishment. We ran three full marathons in 84 days; nobody could take that accomplishment from us. I still like to brag about that one. Most people tell us were crazy for doing that. Well, that is why it is called the Marathon Maniacs and they call it admitting you into the insane asylum.

They always say in your first year running marathons that you shouldn't run more than one. I always had to break the rules. In my first year, I ran four full marathons and a couple of half marathons. I also did the New Town Triathlon and I did an Olympic distance triathlon in Litchfield, Illinois. I felt amazing and I was absolutely addicted to racing. I wanted to do them all. I wanted to do more and try different distances.

Chapter 25

2014- Going a New Distance

I had done half marathons, full marathons, Olympic distance triathlons and the next distance was a half Ironman. That is a 1.2 mile swim, 56 mile bike ride and a 13.1 mile run. I absolutely had to do it. I signed up to do Ironman Muncie in July. I started training and I really had no idea what I was getting myself into. I paid for a customized training plan but I didn't have the money to pay for coaching. I started training and I just dove right in. I was so motivated and I couldn't wait. I could just picture myself crossing that finish line.

As I was training, I signed up for some other races along the way. I did an Olympic distance triathlon in May. I also did a couple half marathons. I ran the Rock n' Roll half in Nashville. In June, I went to San Diego to run the Rock n' Roll Marathon. I got a PR of 2:03 but I am still hoping to get less than two hours sometime soon. I am so close. It was neat going out there because I have a lot of family that lives there and they were able to cheer me on. Any race that Kingston goes to, I always run off the course to give him a big kiss. He is my good luck charm. Kingston, my mom, dad, Aunt, Uncle, and cousins were all at the San Diego race holding up signs for me. I gave Kingston a kiss and then I kept on running.

I had been training for my half Ironman religiously. I would train up to twelve hours a week. I had no problem getting up at four or five in the morning to workout. In fact, that is my favorite time to train. I love starting my day off right. A lot of people don't understand the amount of time and dedication it takes to train for big races, especially when you are training for three different disciplines. It does take away from your social life, but I would rather go to bed early and get up early to train. I would rather wake up feeling good. I don't see the need to go out or stay out late. I am completely over that stage of my life. Triathlons are my drug now.

I was so motivated and I just couldn't wait. It was finally time for my first half Ironman. I spent all of those months training for this one day. My two best friends were going with me to cheer me on. We loaded my bike up on the back of my friend's car and we hit the road. It took a little over five hours to get there. I had no idea what I was doing. I thought I was prepared. It was a completely new accomplishment. I couldn't wait to complete it. When we arrived, I got all checked in. The nerves were kicking in, bad. I ate my pasta dinner and I tried to get a good night's sleep. It is hard to sleep the night before a race. I get so anxious and excited for the next day.

I woke up early that morning. I arrived around 5:30 A.M. and I set up my transition area. I laid down my son's Scooby Doo towel to put my things on. I bring it to every race as my good luck charm. After I got all set up, I used the bathroom as many times as possible before the race began. I sat with my friends and I just tried to stay calm. It felt like the longest wait ever. It was finally my time to get into the water. The swim was in Prairie Creek Reservoir. Even though I am a good swimmer, I stayed back a little. My anxiety gets so bad it is hard for me to settle into breathing. It was time to go. I started swimming. I can't even tell you the thought going through my head as I made that swim. I was hit and kicked in the face but I kept going. I was afraid to get to the end because that meant I had one leg finished. That meant the race was about to begin. I finally got to the end of the swim and I ran out of the water. I felt slightly disoriented as I ran up the path to transition. I saw my friends cheering me on as well as some others who were from St. Louis.

I ran into the transition area and I switched into my bike gear. I dried off and I got ready to go out. It was my weakest portion of the triathlon and it always makes me the most nervous. My transition was a little slow as I was afraid I would forget something. I headed out and I passed by my friends again as I clipped into my bike. I started out on my 56 mile journey. I felt good as I pedaled along but I always get nervous being around other cyclists who are more skilled than me. I also get scared of sharp turns. Everything was going well and I just kept on pedaling. We did a loop where we went out and back, then out and back again. It was a perfect, mostly flat course. I finished the bike portion and all that was left was the run. I only had 13.1 more miles to go.

I ran into the transition area and I re racked my bike. I switched into my running shoes. I couldn't feel my legs. I started running and I remember running by my friends again. They were holding up a sign that said: "Don't Trip." I couldn't help but laugh at their sarcasm. I had a tendency to trip and fall when I was running. It has only happened a few times but, of course, I will never live it down. Once I could feel my legs again, I felt like my run started out great. I wanted to run as much as I could and only walk at water stations. That worked for a while but towards the end I was running for a little bit and then walking for a little bit. I was mad at myself for walking because it was totally mental. I was fine and I could have run.

As I got closer to that finish line, I just couldn't believe it. This was a whole new accomplishment for me and this represented so much to me. It was such an emotional experience and I couldn't believe that I was able to do it. Running across that finish line was an indescribable experience. I finished my first half ironman in 6:45:44. This was just the warm up. I was signed up for another half Ironman in October in North Carolina. After this race, I was on a high for the rest of the day. The high from racing is so much better than drugs.

My first half Ironman was complete and my short weekend trip came to an end. It was time to drive home the following day and head back to reality. It was all I talked about for a week or so. I couldn't wait to tell everyone everything about my race. I felt as if I had bragging rights. I couldn't wait to do it again.

I decided to find a coach to help me prepare for my second race of this distance. I didn't want help with everything. I just really wanted to improve my bike. I reached out to Samantha with Team Evolve. She said it would be better to work on everything as a whole and not just the bike. I thought I had everything else figured out but I decided it was a good idea and there was always room for improvements. Oh, man, my life changed after that. I love the accountability and the feedback on all of my workouts. My logs are like my journal entries where I can vent. I have good training days and I have bad training days. I have learned so much and I feel as if everything as a whole has improved. My coach is absolutely amazing and she always goes above and beyond to help all of the athletes she works with. She is awesome at what she does.

A lot changed in this time period. I quit my job at Silver's gym. It was so stressful for me and I would always get really bad anxiety there. I just think because of how crowded it gets and I felt intimidated. I was constantly having panic attacks and sometimes they would be set off just by things being out of order. I was unhappy and I barely got to see my son. I felt like a weight had been lifted off of my shoulders when I left there. I met some awesome people there but it was just not the job for me. I went back to working full time at King Burger. I always somehow end up back at that place and I have now been there nine years. I do plan to get another job at some point but I will get into that soon. I have been at King Burger so long that it is like my second family. I have worked with some of the same people the whole time. They have watched me go through all of it. They were always there and they always had hope in me. I was spending all of my time working, training and spending time with Kingston. I loved being able to be there in the evenings with Kingston. It also took a lot of stress off my dad because he didn't have to watch him every night.

My training for my next race was peaking. Some days I would have more than one workout and I spent my days off working out for four to five hours sometimes. It was stressful and overwhelming at times but I loved it. Some weeks it would add up to twelve hours' worth of working out in one week. I was noticing the improvements and I couldn't wait for my race. I had way more confidence in my abilities and my coach always believed in me even when I didn't believe in myself. I did a couple other races along the way until it was finally time for my "A" race.

The time had finally come to pack up and head out for my race. This time my whole family was going. It was the end of October and it was in North Carolina. I chose that race because my sister lives there and I wanted to go see her and my nieces. We left at the crack of dawn. We had the car packed and my bike on the back. We set out on our fourteen hour drive. Kingston did awesome being in the car for that long. We stopped a lot on the way down. We got there late that night.

The next day I was able to go check in for my race. I had to leave my bike there which made me super nervous. I began freaking out and having a panic attack about leaving my belongings. I felt like it took my control away and it was put into someone else's hands. I called Samantha and she helped to calm me down. I briefly checked out the course and tried to get an idea for what I was getting myself into. It was a bit of a weird set up. We left there after I was all checked in and we went to eat dinner. I had to load up for my race. My mom and I stayed in a hotel closer to the race. It was about an hour from my sister's house. They didn't come because they had the three kids and my niece had a soccer game. It would have been a lot for all of the kids. My mom was there to be my Sherpa (helper) and cheer me on. She was new and I had to teach her the system. I laid everything out in the evening that I would need for the morning. I went to bed early and I woke up early.

I was so full of emotions and excitement was one of them. I had been waiting for this day for so long and I felt more prepared than ever thanks to my coach. We arrived to the race location early. I put together the finishing touches in my transition area. I just made sure that everything was in the right order and I was not missing anything. I double checked to see where my transition was located from the area I ran in to get to my bike. After going to the bathroom a number of times, I put my wetsuit on. My mom was not the best at helping me squeeze into it, so I had some random strangers help me. That is the best thing about triathletes. They are just a different breed of people and everyone is so friendly. I love the whole race experience and all of the people I have met. I never feel judged.

I had to leave my mom and take a shuttle over to the beach. That wait felt like the absolute longest wait ever. Finally, it was my time to get into the water. It was hard treading water with the current pushing you forward. We had to keep scooting back to make sure we were in the right spot. Then, it was finally time to go. I started up front this time and I was not holding back. The only thing I really struggle with is sighting in open water. I still had an amazing swim. In fact, I dropped ten minutes off the time from my last swim. My swim time was 30:53. This race is also known for having one of the fastest swim courses since the current is with you the whole way. I reached the beach and I ran out of the water. I had a wetsuit stripper help me remove my wetsuit and I ran through the shower area. I had to wash off since it was a salt water swim. In longer races chafing is bound to happen, but I am sure having extra salt on you wouldn't help to prevent it. I ran up towards transition and I saw my mom on the way.

It was a long, slightly uphill transition. It seems most races do this with their transitions. I ran into transition and I found my bike. I dried off and I switched to my bike gear. I ran my bike out of the transition and I saw my mom as I clipped into my bike. I went out onto the course. It went down some main roads and pretty far out. It seemed pretty lonely as we got farther out, no spectators. I got passed by a lot of people and I passed a few people. I had a million thoughts going through my head and I was feeling determined. On the way back, I stopped at the porta potty to use the restroom. I went as fast as I could in hopes I didn't lose time. I clipped back in and I pedaled to the finish. I saw my mom as I rode my bike in. The second transition area was in a different location. I ran in and the volunteers took my bike from me. I went and grabbed my bag with my run gear and into the changing tent. It was in a convention center. I felt I had a fast transition and I headed out for the run.

I felt amazing on the run and I had the goal of not walking. I think I did a little bit but not much at all. I mostly just walked at the water stations. I told myself to stand tall and keep on running. One of my mantras is, "It doesn't matter how fast or slow you go, just keep running and moving forward." Also I always tell myself I will get there faster if I run. I felt very strong on the run. I was getting close to the end. I ran in and I crossed that finish line. My run time was 2:20:32. It was another emotional experience for me and I was on a major endorphin high from the race. I couldn't wait to see what my time was.

When I saw my time I was shocked. I had dropped thirty minutes off my time from my last race, coming in at 6:15:37. I owe major credit to my coach for that and the hard work I put in. She believed in me when I didn't always believe in myself. I collected another medal and I felt that same sense of accomplishment. No words can describe the emotions I feel at the end of each race.

I have used triathlons as a part of my recovery. When I talk about doing a full Ironman, I can't even describe exactly what it means to me. Becoming an endurance athlete has taught me so much about life. I have learned self-discipline, determination, and how to persevere. Each discipline represents something different in my life. It is more than just swimming, biking, and running. I have a different way of looking at it. During the swim, you get hit and you get kicked. You get knocked down and you have to fight to stay afloat. I relate it to life knocking you down. No matter how far you get knocked down, you have to get back up. The bike represents determination. It is something I have to work hard at and I still have a long ways to go. Sometimes I get aggravated at the bike and I want to give up, but I don't. I just keep practicing and I am determined to get stronger. When I look at the run portion, I think of it as running towards your problems and facing them head on. I don't see it as running away. That is just how I represent it all to my life. I could write more about this as it is something I am super passionate about. This sport has seriously saved my life and I just can't express all of my passion towards it. I can't wait until the day I cross the finish line at a full Ironman and I hear: "Jamie Stewart, you are an Ironman!"

Chapter 26

Where I am at Today

It has taken me a long time to rebuild my life. I have become a completely different person. Addiction is not just about being clean and away from drugs; it is also changing your behaviors. You have to change the way you think. From time to time, I feel like my addictive mind kicks in. It is hard to explain. I have come a long ways. Many people are inspired by me and I am hoping to inspire people. I try to act like I have my life together, but the reality of it is that my life is just organized chaos.

My son's dad is back in his life. He got married and his wife reached out to me. I was hesitant at first but I was willing to give it a shot. I tried to start it out slowly because I was so nervous. I knew we both made mistakes and it was a bad time in both of our lives. I was able to move past that and give him one last chance. I told him it would be his last chance. He has been clean for a couple years now. We get along just fine and he has been very helpful. I feel it is much easier to keep it that way. He has made a huge effort in being a great dad to Kingston. His wife has also been great and has stepped in and helped a lot. I don't panic when he goes away for the weekend, although it was hard for me at first. I had never really been away from Kingston. I was a bigger baby about it than he was! The most important piece is that my son is happy. It was a little confusing for Kingston in the beginning, but he adjusted quickly. It is still all fairly new, but I am happy that my son can have his dad in his life. I have learned to forgive everyone that has hurt me in my life. I made a lot of mistakes and people forgave me. I know I must do the same and not hold onto anything in the past. In the end, holding onto the past will only hurt me.

I am still working at King Burger nine years later. I do plan to eventually get another job but I just don't know exactly what it is I want to do. I would absolutely love to go back to school and work towards becoming a substance abuse counselor. I have first-hand experience and I feel I could really relate to people going through what I went through. I have a hard time getting jobs because I have felonies on my record. I will have awesome interviews and get job offers, but I get denied because I have those felonies. I wish they could get to know me and what I've done just so I could have a chance. It does get me down sometimes but I won't ever let it hold me back. It just sucks that you are young and make mistakes yet they hold it against you forever. I am hopeful that I will find a career path that I enjoy. I would love to continue to write and make a career out of helping addicts. This is part of the reason I want to get my story out there. I want to show people the changes that I have made. I want people to see where I once was and where I am at now. I understand that not everybody turns their life around but I feel like I should be given a chance and not be denied because of my past. I even tried finding an apartment for Kingston and me one time and that was a nightmare. I got denied everywhere I went because of my background.

I try to always stay positive and keep an open mind in life. I try to find the positive in any negative situation. When I have a bad day I try to find something that makes that day good. I live my life optimistically. My son is my number one priority. I would never want to do anything to jeopardize that. I think about consequences now. I have such an amazing group of support in my life. I have amazing friends and family. Through doing triathlons and being involved with a club/team, I have met some great people. I have a lot of positive people in my life. Endurance athletes are some of the friendliest people I have ever met. So many people have helped me out in ways I can't even explain. I am beyond thankful for that.

I have pretty much stayed single since I have had my son. I needed that time to reflect and learn who I was. This was my first time living sober. I was focused on myself and my son. I spent a good majority of that time as a single mom. I have way higher standards now because it is not only about me anymore; it is about my son, too. I know one day I will find the right person who can be there for both Kingston and I. I refuse to settle for anything less than what we deserve. I have dated just a little bit and I realize it is way different being sober. Every relationship I had in the past was based off of drugs. I never loved myself and I allowed people to treat me badly. Now that I love myself I would not put myself in those types of situations again.

I did finally complete an outpatient program. After I had my son I went back to the same outpatient program I was in before. I tried that out for a little bit but just being there was a trigger. I always saw so many people I knew from the past and I was so used to getting high the whole time I was there. I went to a different treatment center and I finally successfully passed an outpatient program. I got released from my probation a year early in 2013. I am proud to say that the majority of people who I used to get high with are all clean today. I can't even begin to describe the amount of money I spent on drugs, lawyers, court fees, etc. I have spent over $10,000 just on the amount of trouble I got myself into. That doesn't even include the amount of money I spent on drugs each week. I have nothing to show for that today. Now, I struggle just to get by. I am stilling paying towards my four month stay in St. Charles County jail. I had to pay fifty dollars a day for being there. It is not worth it to get into trouble. It is just a waste of time and money that you can't ever get back.

I am far from perfect and I do not think there is such thing as perfect. It has taken me four years to become confident in who I am. I embrace all of my flaws and my imperfections. I started using drugs as my outlet. I thought doing crazy things made me cool and it made me fit in. I just wanted people to like me because I didn't like myself. Now, I love myself and I love who I am. I took it up on myself to heal my own life. I used running as my therapy. I can't describe what running and triathlons have done for my life. I have gained self-confidence. From time to time I feel down or depressed but not like before. I still get anxiety going into large crowds of people and I am slightly socially awkward. I get panic attacks in large groups but I refuse to take medication for that. I have learned to get it under better control with a lot of deep breathing exercises. I have to mentally block everyone out and put myself in a happy place to get away from it. I tend to get panic attacks before starting triathlons. The best part about going to races with people is they help to keep me calm. I don't normally drive myself to races because of how bad my anxiety gets.

I used to be afraid to share my story about my past. It took me a long time to feel comfortable telling people. A lot of people knew but maybe not the full extent. Today I have no problem talking about it or telling anyone. I celebrated four years clean on August 12, 2014. It was the first time I put a big post to social media about it. Some people were shocked to learn what I had gone through. I was afraid I may get negative feedback, but I didn't. I had so many people give me the most positive feedback and I felt so much love. It was amazing for me. Anyone who meets me today would never guess I went through all of this. I like to let people get to know me before I do bring up my past. Many people are inspired and see everything I have overcome. Not everybody knows my full story and that is half the reason I wanted to write my book. I used to feel like people judged me off of my past, but I don't feel that way anymore. I know I made a lot of mistakes, but I am willing to own up to them and move forward with my life. I can't dwell over the past. I truly believe that everything in life happens for a reason.

When I celebrated four years clean, this is what I posted to social media: *Here goes my super long spill my heart post. Never did I think I would be alive to see the age of 26 and never did I think I would be able to say this today, but I am celebrating four years clean from heroin! After multiple overdoses, near death experiences, and being moments away from being pronounced dead, I am happy to say I made it out alive and I am truly happy to be living today. I love my life and I am beyond grateful for my family and friends who stuck by my side and never lost hope in me even though I was on a completely self-destructive path. Although I regret things I have done in the past and there are things I wish I could change, I wouldn't be who I am today if it weren't for my past. Now I can stay positive and look towards my bright future and know that no matter how bad things get, they will never be as bad as they once were. It makes me sick to look back and think of how sick I was. I can honestly say I am proud of everything I have accomplished today and I am proud of the person I have become. Going through these struggles and fighting this battle has made me an extremely strong person. Kingston was my savior and he pushed me to become a better person. Even though I was pissed off I had to spend my pregnancy in jail, I know it was the best place for me to be at that time. At least we were safe. All I want in life today is for Kingston and I to be happy. I would say I am doing a pretty damn good job at accomplishing that. A big part of my recovery has been running, biking, triathlons, and marathons. It is my new addicting hobby but it is way healthier and it has helped keep me clean and turn my life around. Yes, I will admit that I am addicted to doing races but I love the adrenaline from it. People can judge me off of my past if they want. They can look at me differently but honestly I don't care. It has made me into who I am today. I am writing my book and telling my story to show people that it is possible to turn your life around but it is not always easy. So here is to many more years of living clean!*

Today I always try to stay busy. I am always on the go and most people ask me how I do it. I don't like to have much downtime. I am always working, training for races, or spending time with my son. I take my son to soccer, swimming and karate. He loves to go running with me, too. I have completely turned my life around and I am beyond grateful. I have a completely different outlook on life and I am full of joy. It is the little things in life that make me happy today. Just seeing my son smile makes me happy. Looking at things such as the sky and nature makes me feel happy. Today I choose how I feel. I don't let others affect me and I try to always stay positive. I refuse to let others drag me down.

Chapter 27

My Families Perspective

I asked my mom and sister to write a part for this book. I wanted to show people what my addiction was like from their perspective. I wanted them to be able to express their feelings in the situation. This is their real emotions and what they had to deal with on a daily basis. This is their point of view from the outside looking in.

First, here is my mom's story:

My name is DeDe and I am Jamie's mom. Jamie asked me to tell what it was like to be on the other side and live with a heroin addict. My first reaction was Hell, but I thought I should probably go into a little more detail. Here is my story.

Jamie always seemed like a happy, go lucky young girl with a zest for life. She loved to play sports and spent most of her time playing outside or at the pool. She was basically a normal child and had a normal family life. She was pretty much a tomboy and lived in her soccer shorts and T-shirts when she was not in her swimsuit. During her fifth grade year the district changed the schools. They made grade school K-5 and moved sixth grade to middle school. I always felt in my heart that this was where her problems began. She was not yet ready to be in a middle school environment at all. She would have been better off in grade school for one more year. Her sister, who was already in middle school, let Jamie know that kids did not dress in soccer shorts and T-shirts. Jamie really struggled with her identity this year. She floundered about not really sure where she fit in or who her friends were. I believe we bought her three different wardrobes throughout that year as she struggled to find her fit. I am not sure if it was that year she fell into the wrong crowd or just shortly after.

Little by little life was changing as we once had known it. She continued to play sports but slowly her interests changed and she dropped one sport after another. In middle school she began to get into trouble. We didn't see any real issues yet as it was nothing major.

As she started high school, our first big clue should have been when we went to a meeting for sports. They talked about random drug testing and it was something that was optional. Jamie immediately made a comment that she refused to pee in a cup. We just blew it off and thought it was a modesty thing since she was always shy. That was a big mistake.

Her freshmen year went downhill. She began getting into trouble a lot at school. She would get many in school suspension as well as out of school suspensions. We had her in counseling and working with a psychiatrist. We started looking into other options for schooling such as: home schooling, sending her away for school, and the alternative school. At this point we were just struggling on what to do. She began at Hope High and managed to graduate. At this point, I believe she was beginning to dabble in a lot more drugs than just smoking pot.

Living with Jamie became harder and harder. It was an emotional roller coaster for her and the family. We walked on eggshells around her a lot to keep from rocking the boat. She was emotionally unstable and we feared she would take her life. It caused a lot of friction with her sister as she felt we didn't discipline the same. There was constant turmoil in our house. We feared for our safety, also. We slept with our door locked at night and we were truly afraid of her. She had so much hate for us that if looks could have killed; we would have been dead many times. Through it all, we continued to support her and seek help. We were at our wits end. It would have been so easy to kick her out and wash our hands of her, but we loved her and we wanted to find the Jamie we once knew.

I prayed a lot. Every time she walked out the door I was afraid it would be the last time I saw her alive. If I called her and couldn't get a hold of her I would panic. I can't even describe the feeling of fear that takes over your body. I would become this crazed person. I would call her endlessly, drive around looking for her and call all of her friends. I couldn't sleep until I heard from her and knew she was alive. One day a friend of my sisters suggested that I try her church out. I will never forget that day. I went to her church for the first time and the whole service was about drug addiction. They had a panel of teenagers talking and acting things out. I knew God was talking to me and letting me know he was with me. I seriously bawled through the whole service. It felt so good to know God was there and I continued to go weekly.

This was a very hard time in our lives. It took both her dad and I together to get through it. We leaned on each other a lot. I could not imagine going through this alone. We needed each other. Even though we didn't always agree, we had each other to vent and cry to. I thank Rick for being my rock because I wasn't always strong. I had no idea how bad things truly were but I knew they were getting worse. Her sister would share with us the things she felt we needed to know. We still struggled with what to do or where to turn.

I will never forget the first time Jamie had to go to court because she had been arrested for selling drugs. We sat there all *morning listening to one case after another. They were mostly drug related. The prosecuting attorney was tough and he seemed to think everyone should be locked up and the key thrown away. As the morning went on, Jamie had not yet been called to the stand. We were hoping they would break for lunch as it got later in the afternoon. Finally, Jamie was called and it didn't go very well. She received four months in the women's prison for a treatment program. I will never forget this day as long as I live. I felt like I was punched in the stomach. We didn't even get to hug her goodbye as she was taken away in handcuffs. I sat in that court room and I cried like a baby. That was one of the worst days of my life. I remember how horrible it was to go visit her in jail. It made me feel so dirty. Her niece came to visit and the only way she would get to see her was in jail. It was devastating to take a four year old to see her Aunt in jail. She was there for two weeks and got to come home for a little bit. She then had to turn herself back in for her four months in treatment. As hard as it was for her to be gone, it was also very calming. I didn't have to constantly worry about where she was and what she was doing. I knew she was safe and I knew she was alive.*

She did her four months and I believe it wasn't long after she was released that she was back to her old ways. Once again our life went back to how we knew it. We all continued on working and fighting the daily pressures of having a drug addict in the house. I could continue on for days about what it was like living with her.

Fast forward just a little bit. I vaguely remember the day Jamie told me she was pregnant. I don't know if I was in shock or just worried. It scared me for her to bring an innocent child into this world. I had hoped she had stopped using drugs, but this was not the case. She spent the last four months of her pregnancy in jail. I was angry about it at first, but I knew it was for the safety of the baby.

The day that Kingston was born was such a joyous day. I will never forget when he finally was born. I remember looking up at Jamie and seeing the tears she cried. I want to believe they were tears of joy, but I think there were a lot of different emotions that took over her body.

Kingston was a true gift from God! I am grateful every day for what Kingston has done for our lives. Since coming into this world he has brought so much joy to our family. Most importantly, he gave us back our daughter. I am forever grateful for everyone who supported us and was there to listen to the struggles we were going through. We never hid our problems, but many people had no idea of the severity of our problems. I thank God for being there with our family and helping us through this healing process. I hope someday I can get over the fear that overcomes me when I don't hear from her. It is something that will continue to take time. Even though she had been clean over four and a half years, it will still take time for us to continue to heal and grow as a family. I want to apologize to Brittany for all that she had to deal with as a teen. I thank her for being such a strong person and speaking up. She sometimes had to reel me into reality. Jamie, I am so proud of you and the person you have become. I wish you so much happiness and success. I hope that if your story can change just one life, then you have persevered!

I love you all, God bless!

Next, here is my sister Brittany's story:

I was seventeen and Jamie was fifteen the first time I went to my parents and told them, "Jamie has a drug problem." She started with what I would call "normal" drug experimentation of just a high school student experimenting with weed. That had been going on for some time. I never told my parents about it. To be *honest I didn't think it was a big deal. Most of my friends were trying it. Even I had tried it. It was when she told me she had tried cocaine and meth that I went WHAT? It was a secret I could no longer keep. I remember my dad didn't believe it. I remember my mom crying. I remember feeling so helpless. They took her to counseling and put her in an outpatient rehab program. It did nothing. The doctors diagnosed her with bipolar disorder and placed her on medications. Well medications do not work correctly when you are still using drugs and withdrawal from drugs can look a lot like bipolar disorder. I tried to explain that to my parents many of times. Nothing changed or got better.*

A year later I went away to college. The summer after my freshman year I married my husband who had enlisted in the Marine Corps and was getting back from his first deployment. I knew the drug use was still going on, but at that point I had zero sympathy. I had a hard time understanding it was a disease. I had grown up a lot and been through a lot in the year that I left home. Dennis had gone through his first combat deployment. I felt he was fighting for our country and my sister was choosing to throw her life away on drugs. At that point, I felt it was a choice and I couldn't understand the addiction. I remember October 2009 my dad called to tell me she had overdosed on heroin. I didn't even realize she was using heroin. She used to always tell me she could never shoot something into her veins. It turns out addiction can be pretty powerful and the desperation for the high can make someone do things you never thought they would do. At that moment I still could not understand the disease. I was upset, but still did not have sympathy for her. More than anything I was angry. Dennis was in Afghanistan at the time. He left October 2009 for his fourth combat deployment. It had been the month from hell dealing with the stresses of a deployment. I didn't need the stress of my sister.

August 2010 Dennis, our oldest daughter Camrynn (who was three at the time), and I were in St. Louis visiting family. My sister had recently found out she was pregnant with her son. I was incredibly angry to find out she was pregnant. I thought, "How can you bring a child into the world when you are not even surviving in it?" I knew my sister had a court date for drug related charges. My dad called me in tears. He has always been a tough guy who never showed a lot of emotion. He told me they handcuffed Jamie and she could be spending the next 8 years in jail. Hearing the emotion in my dad's voice and thinking Camrynn will be eleven before she gets to see her Aunt again was hard to think about. Also, thinking my nephew was going to be born in jail was even harder. I remember Dennis and I talking about raising Kingston, at least until she got out and maybe got her life back together. None of us knew it at the time, but Jamie being pregnant and going to jail was the best thing that could have ever happened to her. She did not spend eight years in jail. She spent four months and was released two weeks before her due date. She was clean and she had a reason to live. It was the first time she wanted to change her life. Jamie had to continue a rehab program as a term of her probation. She was not happy with the program and even took it upon herself to find a different treatment program that would help her succeed with sobriety. For the first time in seven years I felt I was getting my sister back.

Through all the years and even to this day I have had a very hard time talking to my parents, more so my mom about Jamie's drug addiction. I felt they were enablers. I know they were so scared of the "what ifs", but I felt she was never going to hit rock bottom. She came home to a nice house, a warm shower and food on the table. They gave her money and bailed her out of jail. She even stole money from them. They always made excuses and had her back. The guilt would consume Jamie. My sister knew right from wrong but the disease of addiction had so much power over her that it didn't matter. Jamie kept a journal. My mom used to sneak into her room and read it to try and understand what she was thinking, feeling, and going through. She had many suicidal thoughts.

I never thought my sister would be alive today, and even more so thriving in life. She has completely turned her life around.

She is a wonderful mother who would do anything for her son. She has a drive to get an education and to better her life, her son's life, and even the lives of others. I am beyond thankful to have my sister back. Even during the beginning of her sobriety we had a very rocky relationship. It wasn't until recently my sister told me she was mad at me for telling. It was something I always kind of knew, but was so thankful to hear the words. I felt for me those words were almost closure to her past. I know I did the right thing by speaking up. It was one of the hardest things I have ever done but the best thing I have ever done. I know it took many more years of addiction and heartache before we got Jamie back but I am so thankful she is back and better than ever!

It is hard for me to read that today. It is hard for me to see what I actually put my family through. I will always feel guilty for the amount of pain I caused them. I can't dwell on everything that I did though. As a family we must all move past it. We can no longer live in the past and relive that. I think between me writing my book and my family writing their piece, this has been a cleansing process for all. It is time to fully move on and let it go. We can't do anything to change what has already happened.

Epilogue

It has not been easy for me to write my story. It took me back to a very dark place. I realize the pain that my self destructive path caused my loved ones. It showed me how much I did wrong. It feels good to release my inner demons. I regret many things I have done and there are things I wish I could change. It doesn't matter, though; what's done is done. I can't go back and change anything in my past. Instead, it was a learning experience that has shaped me into the person I am today. I could tell you a million more stories of the crazy and messed up things I did in my life. I could write a book over a thousand pages of the morally wrong things I have done in my life. I picked out the stories that stood out the most to me and showed what addiction is really like. I tried to leave out as many people as I could and not tell their story. This is my story. I wanted to stay away from glorifying my past. I didn't want to sugarcoat anything in my addiction. It is all the truth and I wanted to give an idea of what it is like to struggle with addiction. It controls you and turns you into a different person.

It goes to show that you should never judge a book by its cover. Be kind to everyone that you meet. You don't know what a person's story is or what they have been through. You never know what each person has overcome in their life. Everyone has a different story and you should embrace others for their differences.

I am proud of everything I have accomplished since I have been clean. It has taken me a long time to rebuild my life. It has taken a long time to regain trust and mend broken relationships. I hurt many people, especially my parents. I feel like it is hard to have a super close relationship with them because I feel I have done so much wrong. I pushed them so far away. I am grateful that I have so many supportive people in my life. I have amazing friends and family who never lost hope in me, even in my darkest times. It is still hard for me to think about the past and all of the hurt that I have caused. I must move forward from it and live in the present and work toward a bright future.

Again, it was hard for me to write my story. I am putting it out there for the world to see. I know people will judge me. I know some people will be shocked to learn more about my past. I have put myself in a vulnerable state and I am letting the whole world in. I do not care if people feel it is necessary to judge me. Everyone has some sort of past but not everyone brings it to light. It is not who I am today. It has pushed me and taught me to be a stronger person. It has taught me to live my life with a new perspective. I try to always stay positive and know that things will never be as bad as they once were. I will never go back to that place.

People ask me how it is today staying clean and if I still think about it. I will say it is something that will be a lifelong battle. Sometimes I see things that will trigger my addict thought process. Sometimes even a song or something so simple can bring back memories. One day I was riding my bike and there was a syringe in the bike lane. It gave me that nauseous feeling, palms sweaty. It took me a few minutes to shake it off. I then thought about everything I had accomplished and I thought about my life today. That bike ride ended up being the best bike ride ever. I was so determined to push myself as hard as I could. I took that trigger and I used it as motivation.

The answer is, yes, I still think about it. I still have triggers but it doesn't happen nearly as much. The more time that passes, the easier it gets. If I ever think about using, I think of the consequences, which is something I never did before. There are only two things that happen to addicts: prison or death. This statement is true and I know it. I think of how quickly everything I have worked so hard for could be taken from me with just one use. I think of my son and how badly that would hurt him. I would never want to lose him over my bad choices. The thought of that kills me inside.

It is crazy to think about what some of my triggers are. It is the smallest things and it can happen randomly at any given moment. There are certain places that trigger me just by driving by them. I do not like to drive to the city because sometimes just being in that area brings up way too many memories. It gives me anxiety being down there and a lot of events for my triathlon club are down in that area. Most of the time I am fine with it, but I never know when it will bother me. It can be little things such as: the weather changing, certain songs, or seeing veins in people's arms. When I got to the doctor and I have to get blood drawn, that can sometimes be a trigger for me. These are just a few of the things that can bring thoughts into my head. Today they are just thoughts and I do not get that craving like I used to. I think of how far I have come and I do not miss the drugs at all. It makes me sick to think about them.

The things that have helped me to get clean are my son and running/triathlons. My son was my savior, my gift from God. He saved my life. I try to keep myself busy training for races. I love all the people and the adrenaline rush that I get from it. It has been a huge part of my recovery. I also love saying the serenity prayer to myself in tough times. Another thing that inspires me is listening to Matisyahu's music. It is a crazy obsession but his music has helped me so much. I can relate the lyrics to my life so much that I feel as if he is speaking to me. He has inspired me. I always listen to him when I work out and it keeps me moving forward always. It keeps me fighting through the pain even when I want to give up. When I listen to the song, "Live like a Warrior," I feel as if it is a representation of my life. I can relate every aspect of my life to that song as well as many other songs of his. Honestly, his music has helped me more than I can even explain to people.

Through my addiction I had no plans for my life. I didn't care if I lived or died. I had no goals and zero ambition. Today I have so many goals. There are so many things I want to do in my life. My number one goal in life is to make sure my son is happy and that he has everything he needs. If he is happy, then I am happy. So far I would like to believe that I am succeeding at that. I also so badly want to complete a full Ironman. I constantly think about it. An Ironman to me represents fighting to the end, overcoming struggle, and winning the battle. It is a representation of my life. I would love to go to Kona Ironman one day as a participant or even as a spectator would be amazing. I would love to qualify to run the Boston Marathon one day. There are so many things I want to do with my life. Most of all, I want to inspire people to live their life to the fullest. I want to inspire people to stay positive and go after their goals. Always dream big. No goal is too big.

It is hard to explain addiction to people who have not been through it. Addiction can happen to anyone. I grew up in a good home and my parents taught me right from wrong. I was a straight A student and I did exceptionally well in school. I was athletic and I participated in activities. I just happened to be in the wrong place at the wrong time. I was a troubled soul who just wanted to fit in.

I am so thankful that I wake up feeling good and refreshed each day. I am no longer worried about where I will get money to get high or how I will go get drugs. Now, I think about what Kingston and I can do together to have fun. I also think about how I will fit my workout in. Sometimes that means getting up extra early to get it done before Kingston wakes up. I enjoy each day and I embrace each day that I am alive. Every morning when I wake up and I take a breath of fresh air, I think about how thankful I am. It is a miracle that I am even alive today, literally. Every time I look into Kingston's big blue eyes, I know that I did something right. I don't know where I would be without him and what would've happened to me had he not come into my life. He is the reason I am living and thriving today. I always wonder if it wasn't for him if I would even be alive right now. All I know is that everything in life happens for a reason and I am grateful for that.

I want to help other addicts to get clean and live happy lives. Quitting heroin is one of the hardest things I have ever done in my life and it makes everything in life seem easy. A lot of people don't ever get clean or don't live to tell their story. Heroin controls you and it changes who you are. Not only do you want the drug, but you physically need it. The withdrawal is painful. It is hard to make it through that. You feel like death. It is hard to even explain the addiction. Only those who have been through it can fully understand it. While it is not easy to do, I am here to tell you that it is possible. You can do it. I want to spread awareness and show people that they can do it. It breaks my heart to know how many young kids are out there suffering from a heroin addiction. I am constantly seeing new stories of young kids overdosing because of heroin. It is the devil's drug. It gives me the chills every time I read of someone losing their life to heroin. I wish I could help everyone and stop this epidemic. I am lucky that I lived and I can tell my story today. I just pray that I can touch someone else's life. I want to spend my life trying to put heroin to a stop and save lives, but I am only one person. Heroin kills!

My Words of Advice

Throughout my addiction I always had a guilty conscience. When I did bad things that I knew I shouldn't, I would feel bad. My parents instilled good values in me. The things I did were out of my character. It was not me; it was the drugs. They controlled who I was and what I did. They were my best friend and my worst enemy.

My parents did everything they could to help me. There was nothing anyone could have done or said to make me change. I was who I was and I didn't pretend to be anyone else. I had to learn on my own. I had to hit rock bottom. Nobody could help me or get through to me no matter how hard they tried. That is the problem with addicts. We have to find out for ourselves. We don't listen to what people have to tell us.

My parents were my enablers. They didn't know they were and they didn't mean to. Every failed attempt to help me just pushed me further and further away. My advice to anyone going through this with their loved ones is to show them tough love. Don't help them pay their bills so they can spend their money on drugs. I was working two full time jobs to support my habits and I could barely pay my bills. When they are working yet they have no money, this is your first red flag. Beware of the mastermind manipulating.

I believe that treatment is the best option. I think twenty-one days in treatment is a great start, but it is not long enough. I find that a long term treatment program would be the most beneficial to anyone suffering. Three weeks is just enough time to clear your head. When you have been an addict for multiple years, a few weeks is not going to be enough to change you. I personally think six months to one year is the best option. When most people look at being gone that long, they do not like it. I see it as a matter of life or death. You can spend time away getting better or you could be gone forever. Which would you choose? I hate to make this statement so depressing, but it is the reality of it. The majority of people that overdose and die do it after getting out of a shorter stint in rehab. That is how I almost died.

If they get arrested, don't bail them out. Let them sit. By doing so, you are enabling them. I know it is hard as they plead for your help. No matter what you love them and you want them safe. Sometimes being locked up can be the safest place for your loved ones. It shows them they can do whatever they want but you will always be there to rescue them. I know it is hard but I am serious: you have to show them tough love.

It is hard to say what to do in the situation of dealing with an addict. Each person is different and deals with addiction in a different way. I wish I could help change everyone. I wish I could tell my story to addicts and It would automatically make a light bulb go off in their head. That is not the case though. Anytime people told me to change or that I was throwing my life away, well I just didn't care. Yes, I wish I would have listened to them. I didn't, though. There is only so much you can do and as one person there is only so much I can do to help. Heroin is one of the most highly addictive drugs. Unfortunately, the success rate of getting clean isn't very high. I want to change those statistics, though. It is possible and I know if we all work together we can do something about this heroin epidemic that has stormed the nation.

This is just my advice based off of my personal experience. I have been on the inside and the outside of addiction. I can tell you the best I can what it is like, but it is hard for anyone who has not been there to understand. Always look for the warning signs. Watch out for track marks and wearing long sleeves when it is hot outside. The nodding out and the pin dot pupils. You have to watch out for the attitude and the loss of interest in activities. Also, when their money starts suddenly disappearing or, better yet, when your money and valuables come up missing. I hate to put it that way but I don't want to sugarcoat it. There is help out there and don't be afraid to ask for it. You would be surprised how many people can relate. I know it is hard. I still feel absolutely horrible for putting my family through everything that I did. I just want you to know that is possible to get clean. I would love to help anyone that needs help in dealing with this. Never lose hope.

Made in the USA
Lexington, KY
21 June 2015